I NEED THEE

True Inspirational Stories of a Problematic Past That Turns Into a Purposeful Future

JACQUIE C. HAMILTON

Text Copyright © 2021 by Jacquie C. Hamilton

All rights reserved. No part of this publication may be reproduced, distributed, or transmitted in any form or by any means, including photocopying, recording, or other electronic or mechanical methods without the prior written permission of the publisher. For permission requests, solicit the publisher via the address below.

SUSU Entertainment LLC
P.O. Box 1621
Cypress, TX 77410
www.susuentertainmentllc.com
susuentertainmentllc@gmail.com

Printed in the United States of America
Library of Congress Cataloging-in-Publication Data

Name: Hamilton, Jacquie C., Author

Title: I Need Thee | Subtitle: True Inspirational Stories of a Problematic Past That Turns into a Purposeful Future | Summary: A journey of a 40-year-old woman that feels trapped in a child's body, a heartfelt and inspiring story of strength, love, and forgiveness

Identifiers:
ISBN: 978-1-956292-05-3 (Paperback)
ISBN: 978-1-956292-06-0 (Hardcover Case Laminate)
ISBN: 978-1-956292-16-9 (Hardcover Jacketed Case Laminate)

Subjects: Biography | Non-Fiction | Pain to Purpose | Reclaim Your Power | Forgive

Book Cover Design © 2021 by SUSU Entertainment LLC

Book Photography by Jacquie C. Hamilton

DEDICATIONS

I love my son, he changed me
If it wasn't for him, I don't where I would be
I remember holding him for the very first time
Thinking to myself, there's no way he could be mine
But he was and I loved him even before he was born
Before him I felt empty, like my heart had been torn
Now I have a reason, I had forgotten how to smile
Nothing brings me more pleasure than being with my child

I love you Jalen,

Mama

Life can be tough, so you must be tougher
The road might be rough, so you'll need to be rougher
You are diamonds, go on and shine
Don't let nothing stop you, because you're girls of mine
Nobody will give it to you, so they can't take it away
You'll earn it I know, because you were raised that way
Stay humble and always lend a helping hand
And remember to be there for one another, whenever you can
I love you and you mean the world to me
May God continue to bless you Just J's, My 3

I love you Jakyah and Jamaykah,

Mama

TABLE OF CONTENTS

Chapter One
Reminisce On the Good Times

Chapter Two
There's Nothing like Spending Time with Grandma

Chapter Three
When Praises Go Up Blessings Come Down

Chapter Four
The Day My Life Changed for the Worst

Chapter Five
Feelings of Hopelessness and Helplessness

Chapter Six
You Are Beautiful and Worthy

Chapter Seven
Teachers Are Our Heroes

Chapter Eight
Wherefore Art Thou My Husband?

Chapter Nine
Forgiveness in the Eyes of God

Chapter Ten
Help a Friend in Need

Chapter Eleven
Unplanned Parenthood

Chapter Twelve
Autism Strong Mom

Chapter Thirteen
Parental and Societal Rejections

Chapter Fourteen
Blessings in the Midst of the Storm

Chapter Fifteen
911, What Is Your Emergency?

Chapter Sixteen
My Daughters Are My Angels on Earth

Chapter Seventeen
Don't Let Others Define Who You Are

Chapter Eighteen
Take Control of Your Mental Health

Chapter Nineteen
All We Need Is Love

Chapter Twenty
Big Battles and Bigger Blessings

INTRODUCTION

"I Need Thee" is a personal faith-based expression you say when life throws you into complicated situations and you need to be rescued. As a child, we sing, dance, laugh and play. We have hopes and dreams for our lives, but we never think about the challenges that we may have to face. Our faith may be tested over and over again. The stresses of life can affect our mental well-being, how we think, feel, and act at every stage of our lives. No one can determine what obstacles we will endure. It is very important to love ourselves, know our self-worth and maintain self-care.

"I Need Thee" is for a single Mom who may not know where she will get the money to buy food for her children's next meal. A husband that has been laid off and his medical insurance is ending. Sadly, he can't find the words to tell his wife, who is getting ready to have their first child, or a foster child that has constantly been placed in abusive foster homes, "I Need Thee." Whatever you are going through it is temporary and God will always be there to help you ease your pain. No matter your story, always pray and never give up, even when your journey gets hard, because God may be pushing you into your destiny.

For quite some time, I have wanted to tell my story because I felt that it would give my life meaning well beyond what I could ever imagine. Through my life's journey, I have felt like a grown woman trapped in a child's body. Many people go through adversity and have nowhere to turn and fearful to discuss with others because of how they will be perceived. Sometimes we are afraid to reveal what God wants to heal. Telling your truth isn't always easy, and definitely may be frowned upon, but it is your truth. If you haven't walked in that person's shoes, you cannot judge. Your life doesn't have to be perfection but progress. God will always give us strength through our struggles and a journey of trials into miracles of triumphs. "I Need Thee" is a book of my true reflections of love, strength and forgiveness, as it will guide you to your pursuit of having a happy, healthy, faith-filled life of purpose.

Chapter One

REMINISCE ON THE GOOD TIMES

I have always loved to read, but I often wondered why people would write biographies and tell the world about their most intimate deep dark secrets. The same thing I have feared for so many years, God is giving me the courage to do. We will never know how strong we truly are until being strong is the only choice we have. My life is a tribute to how great God is. Telling our stories can be the best stress reliever in the world. It will give guidance to someone going through the same or similar paths that we've traveled.

There was a time when I was so happy. I remember how fun it was when I was a little girl. We would take trips to the beach, zoo, or to Columbus, Georgia to visit our Dad's brother. We enjoyed spending time together as one big happy family. I remember when Dad got paid, he took me and my three siblings in his truck to pick up his paycheck.

We'd stop at this little country store, and he would buy each of us an oatmeal pie and Coca-Cola. On Fridays we would go to the Movie Gallery and Dad would rent scary movies. Movie Gallery and Blockbuster Video was a popular movie and game rental company where families could rent DVDs, VHS tapes, Blu-Ray Discs, and video games.

I was a true Daddy's girl and, in my eyes, he was my best friend. When I was with him, I felt so free and complete. I know our Dad had some flaws but being around him was better than life itself. He was a very wise man and often I would daydream about having a companion just like him as an adult. There were so many good times with our Dad. I remember how he would sometimes sneak out the back door and pop up at the window and scare us. He was so fun to be around, and he loved playing pranks on us. He had this infectious laugh that would spread to everyone around him.

When we were with our Dad, there were no worries, and although I knew he wasn't a perfect man, being with him we were happy, carefree and loved in a safe environment. It felt like we had the Huxtable's type of lifestyle, the fictitious family on The Cosby Show. We may have not been rich, but the joy and happiness we shared, it was more than money could buy.

As kids just having a parent spend quality time and love you was everything we needed. Dad was a great provider. I remember when we moved into our trailer home, our parents had purchased a washer and dryer and my brother walked in and said, "Wow, we have two washing machines!" Dad thought this was the funniest thing. It was like we had moved on up like The Jefferson's.

I disliked sports but Dad and my big brother Jacob was always watching some type of sporting program. Baseball, football, basketball, tennis and golf, they made it look like so much fun, so I figured if you can't beat em, join em! At first, I was just watching the games because some of the men looked handsome. I really didn't understand what was going on. I used to ask so many questions, but my brother didn't seem to mind, he would answer them all. Basketball ultimately became my favorite sport, especially during March Madness and the playoffs. My brother collected baseball cards, football cards and basketball cards and I would steal some of them. I fell in love with basketball, and I truly admired NBA Hall of Famer Jalen Rose. I knew if I ever had a son, he would share his exact same name.

My Dad wasn't my biological Dad, but he had been in my life since I was 2 years old and was the only Dad that I knew. They say if you feed a child long enough, they will start looking like you. Well, I think that statement has some truth, because I looked like my Mom and especially my Dad. For any man to be an instrument of hope and healing to fatherless homes, they truly deserve praise for their willingness to step in and be a father figure for those who have none. My Dad was everything to me. He was my mentor, caretaker, counselor and friend. He was very easy-going and sensitive to our wants and needs, and always tried to make sure we were all happy.

We lived in a two-parent household and life was good. My Mom, who has a twin sister, was reared in a big family. My Grandma and Granddad was blessed with 12 children in my small hometown of Greenville, Alabama. Greenville is a short distance south of Montgomery, the state capital. A lot of travelers find that Greenville is a great place to eat, shop, and rest right off I-65 on their way to the sandy white beaches of the Gulf Coast. Greenville is known for its rich history, southern charm, and beautiful Camellias, that's why it is known as the Camellia City.

There are so many success stories that have come out of Greenville and the Butler County area. I absolutely love my hometown! It doesn't matter if you are from a small town, success starts in the mind with a lot of hard work. You can't change your past, but you can work towards your future. Taking small steps forward is better than staying in the same place and it will help you decide what you want to do in your life. Always dream big.

My Grandma must have known that my Mom was going to be a beautiful diva, because she had the same name as a makeup collection but spelled differently. She was tall and slender and had the body of a fashion model. I loved to see Mom getting ready to go to an event or a church program, because she would always put on the perfect outfit and her makeup would be so flawless, like she was getting ready to attend a red-carpet premiere.

Growing up Mom often talked about having to work in the fields as a child and having to walk a long distance to catch the bus to school. She had four children and I was the third child. Isn't the number three some sort of lucky number? Or maybe three is a crowd, but either way I made my grand entrance into the world on December 6, 1980, which explains why I absolutely love cold weather. I loved being born in December, close to Christmas, my favorite holiday.

Chapter Two

THERE'S NOTHING LIKE SPENDING TIME WITH GRANDMA

We had to move in with my Grandma for a while, and at the time, her only neighbor was her sister, who lived right next to her on a dirt road. My Grandma had two sisters that she would call and talk on the phone to everyday. Her sister from next door would walk over to her house to talk, especially if they had some juicy gossip to talk about.

For as long as I can remember our families would get together at my Aunt Zuleen's house for the holidays. Christmas was always a special time for us. We had family to come from all over. Some were in the military and traveled from overseas, some flew in from New York and surrounding areas, and others came from right around the corner, but we all would be happy together. I absolutely loved my family. Aunt Zuleen would have a gift for everyone that came in the door, no one was left out. We would have so much food, everything you wanted to eat or thought you wanted to eat was there. All kinds of cakes and pies. My favorite was a jelly cake.

Grandma used to make her special jelly cake and I couldn't get enough of it. As I reminisce about those days, I wish I would have paid closer attention to her and how she cooked and baked from scratch. She was so loving and kind, she was the strongest woman I knew. She taught us that nobody was going to just give us anything in life, we had to work hard for it. Grandma would get her grandchildren that lived with her or nearby and take us to the fields. We would pick peas, butter beans, peanuts and pecans. It would take forever to fill up that five-gallon bucket.

My Grandma believed in sharing with others, she would say, "We will pick on half." I didn't understand what that meant, but after picking up all those crops, and all the time we spent in the fields, when we could have been playing, Grandma would just give some of our buckets away to others. It just didn't make much sense to me, but we did what we were told. When we made it home from the field, we would all get a pan and start shelling the peas or whatever we had picked that day.

My cousins didn't know it, but it was always a race for me. I wanted to be finished with my chores first, not that I was going to win a prize or anything, but I just wanted to be done to say I was finished first. Making the chore a competition seemed to make it more enjoyable and exciting. I remember we use to shell peas and beans while watching Oprah. Grandma didn't miss an episode of The Oprah Winfrey Show, she loved her! We occasionally watched The Rolanda Watts Talk Show. I remember Grandma would say, "Her skirts are too short," but she still supported her because both ladies made a huge impact in the world.

During my Grandma's era you very seldom saw a lot of black people on TV, especially black women. However, she grew up watching Hattie McDaniels, an American actress, singer-songwriter and comedian, who was the first black woman to receive an Academy Award for Best Supporting Actress in her 1940 role as Mammy, in "Gone with the Wind."

Ethel Waters was an American blues and jazz singer. She was the first black woman to appear on radio, and the first black woman to star in a commercial network. She was also the first black actress to star on her own television show and be nominated for an Emmy Award for her guest appearance on "Good Night, Sweet Blues," and an episode of "Route 66."

Josephine Baker was an American-born French entertainer. She was a beloved singer and dancer, the first black woman to star in a major motion picture entitled "Zouzou" in 1934. Josephine was a World-renowned performer and World War II spy. She was also equally known for her work in the Civil Rights Movement, she continued to fight racial injustices into the 1970s.

Dorothy Dandridge is an American actress, singer, and dancer. The first black actress nominated for an Academy Award for Best Actress for her starring role in "Carmen Jones." She was also the first black woman on the cover of Life magazine and still one of the world's most celebrated beauties.

Our generation is most familiar with the iconic, Cicely Tyson, an Emmy and Tony Award winning legend, and for the Outstanding Lead Actress in a Television Movie for her performance in "The Autobiography of Miss Jane Pittman" in 1974. She was also the oldest actress to win a Tony Award for Best Performance by an Actress in 2013, for her role in the play "The Trip to Bountiful."

Black women have been gracing the stage with their talents for many years showing the world that representation does matter. Having diversity in entertainment is important because it brings in more success, promotes inclusion, acceptance and creates more role models to inspire others.

The grandchildren truly enjoyed being at Grandma and Grandpa's house, and they loved having us around. They lived in the country on a dirt road and in the front of their house was a big oak tree in a ditch where we loved to play. We would make a lot of our own things to play with. My brother would make bow and arrows out of sticks and whatever string or rope he could find. He was very creative. We made kites out of newspaper using two sticks tied together like a lowercase "t." We would play baseball with my cousins who lived next door with their Grandma, my Grandma's sister.

Whatever we didn't have for our summer games, we would create. If we didn't have a real ball, we made one and we used a stick for the bat. It was always so much fun with my cousins, they were friends and cousins altogether. As cousins we spent so much time together, it was like we were brothers and sisters. We worked in the fields together, we played together, and on Sunday mornings we went to Sunday school and church together.

My world had been torn to pieces as my Grandma passed away on my birthday in 2000. It was the worst birthday for me, but I eventually decided to change my thinking. Every year I not only celebrate my birthday, but I celebrate my Grandma's too and enjoy reminiscing on the fond memories that she left for our family. Although we miss my Grandma, I am happy that she saw the majority of her grandchildren grow into young adults. She was like sunshine to our souls even through life's ups and downs. I truly miss her and all our bonding time.

I heard that the best part of being a Grandma is that you get to spoil your grandchildren in a way that you couldn't with your own children. Our Grandmother's love turned us into the adults we are today. I remember her being so proud of us, even when we thought it didn't matter, she thought it did. We will always remember the life lessons that she taught us. They may have been old fashioned to some, but in my eyes, they will never go out of style.

Chapter Three

WHEN PRAISES GO UP BLESSINGS COME DOWN

When I was little my favorite part of the entire church service was listening to the choir. When they decided to make a youth choir, my cousins and I joined. I couldn't sing a lick, but my sister Julia, my cousin Phyllis, and our cousin's Kylie, Elijah, and Briana could sing. The funniest thing happened while we were singing one Sunday, my cousin Phyllis was leading praise and worship when all of a sudden, her nose was bleeding profusely.

Thankfully she was ok, but we joked saying, "God had his blood running all through her nostrils." Although I didn't have a talent of singing, I still got up and sung songs of praises in my blue and white choir robe because it made me feel good inside. It was like I had no worries when I worshipped God. I was young and I didn't know much about talking to God, but when we sung, it was like our own little ministry.

Singing in the choir gave you a sense of peace and purpose, no matter what obstacles you were facing. Hearing the tapping of the drums, sweet melodies of the piano, the majestic sounds of the organ, beautiful tones of the sopranos, altos, tenors, and baritone voices all blended had the congregation standing on their feet and clapping their hands. The Holy Spirit was truly in the building, and you knew whatever you were going through everything would be alright. I know God knew our hearts were in the right place.

One of my favorite songs that we would sing in the choir was called "Two Wings" by The Christianaires. When we sung that song the church members would be up rejoicing and singing along. "Oh, I want two wings to veil my face, Lord, I want two wings to fly away, Lord, I want two wings to veil my face, and I want two wings to fly away."

When I was younger, we would go to two churches, my Grandma's church was Mt. Zion Missionary Baptist Church and my Granddad's church was Mt. Olive A.M.E Zion Church. It was like my family was split, some worshipped with my Grandma, and the others with my Granddad. I was a very shy child, but for some reason I enjoyed learning poems and participating in plays for the Easter and Christmas programs.

My Mom reminisced about me reciting The Lord's Prayer when I was only two years old, and although I don't remember it, I'm quite impressed with myself. I'm not surprised, because my family poured church, the Bible, and the love of God into us as children. I remember my Aunt Sharon was our Sunday school teacher and she would ask the question, "Who is God?" She answered, "A spirit that always was and always will be!" Some things you just don't forget. Church played a vital role in my life as a child. I loved watching the adult's fellowship with one another, work in the community together and praise the Most High God as they prayed their stress away. Some of my most prized gifts in my adult life were cultivated from the church.

Chapter Four

THE DAY MY LIFE CHANGED FOR THE WORST

I'm choosing to be open because I believe that showing my vulnerability is powerful, and when you discuss your mess, it turns into your message that will help others gain strength to share their testimony. When I was 11 years old, I got in trouble by my teacher for passing notes to a boy in class. My Mom was contacted, and I was put on punishment. I couldn't go outside and play with my friends, and they couldn't come to my house. One day my Mom and Dad had to go to work, so my Mom asked my uncle to make sure I didn't go outside. My brothers and my cousins were outside playing basketball and my sister was gone with her Aunt Katherine.

I can still remember the conversation like it was yesterday. My uncle asked, "Why did you get in trouble at school?" I replied, "I was passing notes to a boy in my class." He then asked, "Do you like the boy?" I wasn't quite sure where this was going, but I happily replied, "Yes!" He seemed very interested in my likes for this boy, constantly asking more questions.

He went on to ask, "Have you ever had sex before?" I immediately yelled "No!" I had never even kissed a boy, so sex wasn't on my mind at all. My uncle asked, "Do you want to have sex?" By this time, he was sitting next to me on the couch and his eyes were undressing me. He started rubbing my legs and I just sat there as stiff as a board, scared to breathe, scared to blink, scared to say stop. I couldn't believe my uncle, my flesh and blood, would react to me in this way. He made me feel so uncomfortable. I was only 11 years old!

My brother walked up on the porch and my uncle jumped up from beside me. He came inside the house and got some water. I remember trying to beg my brother to stay inside. I begged him with my big eyes. Sometimes my eyes say what I can't or don't say, but he didn't pay attention to any of my gestures. I watched my brother the whole time, hoping and praying he would feel my cry for help, but he didn't, he went back outside to play ball.

Lord, I wanted to scream! Help! I needed my Mom! "I Need Thee!" When my brother left out of the house, my uncle locked the door and grabbed me by my arms and pulled me down the hallway. I stumbled, and tried to push back, when he sensed what I was doing, he stopped pulling and started dragging me on the floor.

He took me into the bathroom with the two washing machines and did what he wanted to do to me. When he was done, he looked me dead in my eyes and said to me, "If you tell anyone, I mean anyone, I will kill you!" He turned around, zipped up his pants, and left me there like a dirty rag left to be thrown away. He took my innocence away. "Why God?" I asked. I hated myself.

I played it repeatedly in my head how I should have reacted differently. I was in total shock that my uncle would do this to me. Why didn't I fight back harder? I attempted to blame myself for my uncle's cowardly behavior. His verbal manipulation, aggressive, malicious act of rape and sexual assault had me feeling broken inside.

He overpowered me and took advantage of me because I was a child. I didn't know what to do, because I was only 11 years old. He went next door to a neighbor's house and started drinking and hanging out with his buddies like nothing had happened. When my Mom got home from work I didn't care what my uncle told me, I got up the courage and immediately told her.

I felt so good to get it off my chest because it was weighing on me, and I was still shaken to pieces. My body had been violated by my uncle, someone I looked up to. I told her, but I couldn't tell how she felt about it. She later told me that she asked him, but he denied it, and that was pretty much the end of the story.

There was no closure for me, the sexual assault played constantly in my head. I felt icky, and unclean because his scent stayed on me in my mind, even after I had taken several showers. I often wondered, why wasn't I protected? Why wasn't he charged by the authorities? I really needed someone to talk to, I needed my Mom. "I Need Thee!" "Does anyone care how little black girls are being treated? Where was the justice for me?" This is happening to boys and girls of all backgrounds across the world.

After feeling less than, sad, depressed, miserable, ashamed, hurt, disappointed and unloved, I became a very rebellious and aggressive child. I did everything I knew I wasn't supposed to do. I hated my family, because they brushed me being raped by my uncle under the rug like it was nothing.

I felt my Mom and family members cared more about the reputation of our family instead of the well-being and love for me. I distanced myself from family gatherings and reunions. How can I pretend that everything is ok, when it is not? Hurt people, hurt people! Did someone violate my uncle as a child? Why would my family continue to entertain this monster when I'm hurting? I felt like I was damaged goods, like bent cans with torn labels that are given away to charity not looked at as good as others, not worthy to be full priced.

Set Me Free

One day I want to be free
I want to be able to tell my story
This hurt I've been feeling, has gotten the best of me
It's making me bitter, mean, and very angry
I run good people off, I just push them away
I say they can go, but I really need them to stay
But I let them leave and I deal with things alone
Every single issue, on my own, one by one
Sometimes I have to cry, when I'm by myself
Then I say, Jacquie pull it together, because I have no one else
I had to be independent, what can I say
Ever since I was younger, I was forced to be this way
Maybe one day I'll be comfortable enough, to let it all go
Maybe, I'm not sure, I guess we may never know

Chapter Five

FEELINGS OF HOPELESSNESS AND HELPLESSNESS

There were many sleepless nights, fears and anxiety attacks. So many young girls and boys that are raped and molested don't have the courage to speak up, but I did! I felt so proud of myself for telling my Mom, my confidant, my protector. I knew that I could tell her anything and she would protect me, but that didn't happen. Some people avoid talking about the dynamics of trauma. In my Mom's eyes, I guess I was supposed to compartmentalize my feelings.

A lot of black families function with the notion that, *our business is our business*. They may say, "Kids will be kids, they were just messing around and didn't know what they were doing." As a result, this type of thinking truly hurts the person that was victimized. My uncle was not a kid, he was a grown man taking advantage of his helpless niece that was on punishment. I love my Mom, but the lack of communication and support from her resulted in emotional distance between the two of us. As a child I felt abandoned inside and completely alone.

I'm A Flower

A rose? A daisy? A lily? No, I'm a cactus
I push people away
I jump when they try and hug me
I'm scared that if they get too close
I'll hurt them and make them bleed
I'm a cactus
I think that I should be alone
Out of everyone's way and not causing harm
But God loves this cactus
You know how I know?
He gives it the sun and the rain
And everything it needs to grow

    Sadly, I have lived in pain mostly all my life because of lack of support. Living with this secret has been eating away at the core of my soul. I go to bed with images of the violation, I wake up with the same images in my head, and it is truly hard to shake it off. What is even more disturbing was how my family could carry on through life like it never happened. This is not ok for anyone to have to function in life this way.

I kept my girls very close to me because I feared that someone would touch them inappropriately. Growing up they never had slumber parties or sleepovers. I wanted to always make sure my girls felt protected. I played it in my head what I would say to my uncle if I ever got the opportunity, but I never confronted him as a child, but I often thought about it. I remember hearing the elders say how you should put your problems in the hands of the Lord and let him fight your battles. I pray and pray but the hurt never goes away. Why would he do something so despicable to his own niece?

I often blamed God for letting this happen to me. I suffered badly in silence. Everything stayed boggled up inside and sometimes I felt like I was about to pop! I felt dirty, used and abused. I didn't know whether my Mom would believe me or not but it was never a topic of discussion. I felt my family thought the best way to handle the situation was to not address it and just get over it. It is not that easy! I had difficulty focusing in school, nightmares, numbness, fear and anxiety, sadness, agitations, aches and pains, lack of support, lack of participation in school activities and making friends. The trauma continued to play in my head, and caused higher levels of stress, ongoing emotional upsets, psychological issues, low self-esteem, depression and eating disorders. I really needed therapy and still do.

Innocent Child

He touched me shhhhh
He hurt me shhhhh
I'm ashamed shhhhh
I want help shhhhh
I can't be quiet, no matter how hard I try
I'm only a kid, I just want to cry
Somebody protect me, take me away
I'm still here, I have to stay
I'm so angry, stay away from me
I feel locked up, but I'm supposed to be free
When I get older, I'm going to change the world
But right now, I'm just a scared little girl

    I truly felt unloved by my family and didn't have love or respect for myself. I was scared to death to tell my Mom what had happened, but I got enough courage to share it with her. I felt so hurt not to get the support that I well deserved. Our bodies are supposed to be sacred, our temple, preserved for our spouse. God wants us to respect our bodies because a healthy body gives us the energy we need to do God's work. I never knew this until I became an adult. If I could only turn back the hands of time and someone would have had open communication with me, I would have taken better care of my body.

Boys started showing interest in me and I began to feel alive again. I started getting attention, but it was all the wrong attention. I started believing that they loved me, but they really were wanting to have sex with me. I was so confused, and I couldn't determine what love was or what it wasn't. I just felt like why not, if someone like my uncle, the person that I have always held to a higher standard do something so disgusting to me, then it shouldn't matter if I let anyone else do it, and so I did.

Sex Is Not Love

He doesn't want me, he just wants what I have
And I gave it to him
I spread my legs opened wide
And I let him in
He doesn't love me, he barely knows my name
But he kept going in and out of me until he came
I'm so ashamed and I'm looking for someone to blame
Sex is not love, but it feels like it when you don't know what love is
He just walked away, didn't even leave a goodbye kiss
One day I hope to find what I am looking for
Until then, every time he knocks, I'm opening the door

My family let me down, so much that I stayed completely away. I was only 11 years old, I had just gotten my period, I couldn't protect myself, and nobody else did either. When I think of a Mother, they are the ones you can talk to about anything, they will always be there for you, no matter the circumstances. I often sat and wondered why this innocent child wasn't protected? I felt failed by the world and especially by my family.

My heart was torn to pieces, I have cried so many tears. *You may be saying, get over it Jacquie, it has been 30 years. You must have lost your mind to bring this up now.* "No, I haven't, but with God on my side, I'm working on finding my peace of mind." I wish it was that easy, to just forget about it, but if you haven't walked in my shoes, you wouldn't understand. If you ask any victim of rape, molestation or sexual assault whether they can recall when they were violated, they will have a vivid memory of the details.

At 40, I see it just like it happened yesterday. This has truly affected me in my adult life, always attracting the wrong guys, not feeling worthy to be loved the right way, and feeling trapped. I have it in my heart to forgive my Mom for not coming to my rescue and my uncle for taking my innocence away but I just haven't taken that step. Help me. "I Need Thee!" Maybe if I forgave them, I would be able to move on with my life and God would bless me with happiness, peace of mind and healthier relationships.

What happened to the happy family me and my siblings once had? I was devastated when my Mom and Dad went their separate ways. Life with both parents gave us the balance and structure that our family needed. I don't truly understand what happened because I was only 12, but I knew that my Mom wasn't happy anymore.

I needed my Dad more than ever before. I had been violated and my Dad had always been my listening ear and true friend, but he wasn't there. I was haunted many days and nights of the images of my uncle attacking me. After my Dad left, my Mom moved on with another relationship and I had more freedom than any 12-year-old child should have. There were no curfews for me, I did any and everything. My Mom was only there physically but she was dealing with other things, and I didn't want to keep being a burden to her.

Unintentionally, I started blaming my Mom for my Dad leaving us and not protecting me from the hurt of sexual abuse. There was so much I was dealing with as a child that I couldn't even process it clearly. I didn't have anyone to discuss what I was going through except my Aunt Naomi. Aunt Naomi would always empathize with me and encouraged me. Besides my Grandma, she was the only one that seem to truly care about my feelings.

She would say, "Prissy write your Mom a letter." My family nicknamed me Prissy as a baby. My Mom always kept me looking neat and clean, and I didn't like to get dirty. I was truly a little princess. I loved my Aunt Naomi because she didn't judge me. She cared about me and wanted me to express my feelings the best way I knew how. I am happy to give Aunt Naomi her recognition because she is a big reason why I didn't completely lose my sanity. She was raising a son and a daughter around the same age as me and always showed me love and empathy.

Chapter Six

YOU ARE BEAUTIFUL AND WORTHY

A Mother's love to her children, especially her daughters doesn't have to come from her purse or wallet. We love our parent's presents but what is most important is their presence. Don't assume that your child loves themselves. Hearing positive affirmations such as, "I love you," "You are beautiful," "You are perfect just the way you are," "You are more than enough," "I am proud of you," builds up confidence.

I had very low self-esteem as a child, and I often wondered in my adult years if my life would have been different if my self-esteem had of been better. You learn through the hardness what love looks like. My Mom's love wasn't conveyed to me through words like I needed it to be. Although I would hear from others tell me that I was pretty, I desired compliments from my Mom. I yearned for her approval. I wanted to know that she thought I was beautiful because I truly lacked self-confidence.

As a child, the real difficulty was to overcome how I felt about myself, but the dialogue between my Mom and I wasn't there. I would get a compliment from others, but in my mind, I allowed negative thoughts to take over and convince myself that they didn't mean it. The emotional, physical, and sexual abuse that I endured had me believing that I wasn't worthy of hearing positive words being spoken about me.

I couldn't shake the feeling off me, because I was always finding myself worrying about the way I looked, always second guessing how I acted, and how people perceived me. I never knew how to be myself. I'm not playing the blame game on anyone, but this unstable behavior has interrupted my entire life as a child, teenager, and in my adult life. I constantly make poor relationship choices, I have insecurities with trusting others, and I never ask for help from others. I struggle with speaking up for myself and learning how to prioritize my wants and needs.

Some may be saying, *that's not the Jacquie that I know*. In public places you would have thought my confidence was above the roof. I never wanted pity from anyone because we all go through disappointments in life. Sadly, I have been proposed to by a few men, but I didn't feel deserving of a good life and true love, so I would find a way to get rid of them. I know that the relationship didn't manifest into a marriage solely because of me not trusting anyone. Please excuse my French but "I am 40 years old and still fucked up!" "I Need Thee!" If you don't have love for yourself, it is hard for you to give anyone else love. This way of thinking isn't easy to understand but loving yourself is not automatic.

My skin complexion was dark, and I felt that I was ugly. I had eyes that bulged out of my head and my hair was kinky. When I was younger, I truly hated the way I looked. In high school, no one seemed interested in me, because most of my male classmates seem to always gravitate towards the girls that were light-skinned with long hair. It was like dark-skinned was demonized but light-skinned was the prize. I often wondered why God created me this way. It is sad that we often fight for justice when other races discriminate against us, but we do it to ourselves. Why do black people discriminate against each other? Society often displays beauty as being a Caucasian white woman with blonde hair and blue eyes or someone with lighter skin.

Colorism is prejudice or discrimination against individuals with dark skin tones, typically among people of the same ethnic or racial group, which may cause you to have emotional and psychological issues. This type of thinking was deeply rooted in racism where someone's value and superiority were based on the color of their skin. The slave master favored the lighter skin tones, often giving them preferential treatment to work in the house, whereas the darker skin tones worked outside in the fields. Not only is being color struck an issue among the black community, but also in other communities around the world.

Sadly, today people face different educational and economic outcomes solely based on their skin color. Our strength is in our wisdom and knowledge. Therefore, it is so important to get an education, read and educate yourself to be all that you can be, no matter what you look like. Don't use the prejudices of the world to limit your abilities to be great.

God has equipped us with everything that we need to be successful. Learn to prove others wrong and don't allow anyone to tell you what you cannot do. I pray that our world can stop having a plantation type of mindset. Treat all people with kindness and respect and focus on having a good character. Let's celebrate ourselves. No one knows what it takes to be you. There is power in your purpose. We must stop the hate amongst each other, love one another, work together and build generational wealth.

Black women are smart, beautiful, resilient, powerful trailblazers and innovators, although we don't always get the credit that we well deserve. We are versatile when it comes to our creativity, this is what makes us stand out in a crowd. Our flawless skin tones, diverse body shapes, and different hair textures is why we are undeniably unique. I decided a long time ago that I would no longer compare myself to others. I am made in God's perfect image, and I am created exactly how I am supposed to be.

I used to feel ashamed of my kinky hair but I am thankful that God has blessed me with so many talents to know how to manage my crown of glory. I've always been good at creating styles for my hair and others, but I was looking for a long-term style where I could avoid putting heat on my hair, a style that would be healthy and easy to maintain. I started cultivating my hair in two strand twists to start the process of locs. At the beginning we go through what I call the ugly stage. This stage is unfavorable among many because it is when we are forming the locs, so our hair is completely out of whack.

During this stage I wore my stylish wigs and everyday someone complimented me on my hair. Some may choose to coil, braid, or palm roll their locs. When my hair finally loc'd people were so amazed at the progress and how good it looked. Locs allow for a range of styling options. We can form braids, twists, set on rollers, put into up-dos and cut into short lengths. I made the choice to embrace my natural hair and I am happy to be living my best loc life!

This Is Me

I hate my skin
I hate my hair
I want to be pretty
It's just not fair
They call me names
And make me feel shame
It's the sun's fault, that's who I blame
But I am pretty
It just took me a while to see
I am not you and you are not me
My hair is like wool, the same as the boss
You know the man that died on the cross
I don't care who judge me, because they judged him too
And he still died for me and for you
So don't look like that, when you see me walk by
Just admire my beauty, because my confidence is extremely high

Not until I've gotten older the things that I hated about myself when I was younger, God has helped me to love. I totally embrace being different. In the lyrics of country singer Mickey Guyton, "The things I did to fit right in. I will never justify my skin. I found my freedom when I learned not to care. Now I'm not scared to love who I am. I love my hair." I still have many struggles that I continue to pray about and work on, but one thing I do know is that my black is absolutely beautiful!

From my smooth hot cocoa melanin-rich skin, big, bold and beautiful brown eyes, vivacious, voluptuous curves, and my lovely, luscious, locs, I am loving the skin that I am in! It is important to always remember that beauty goes beyond your outer appearances. Loving yourself and others is what God wants for us. I am still learning what self-love really means and how to apply it to my daily life.

Self-love is an action not a state of feeling good. It doesn't matter if we get a beauty makeover and new outfits from Gucci, Versace, or Neiman Marcus, although it makes us feel good and is truly gratifying, this is not self-love. Self-love is appreciation of oneself that grows from actions that support our physical, spiritual and psychological growth. When we grow in self-love, we accept our strengths and weaknesses. We lack self-love when we have trouble accepting appreciation from others. Not having self-love will create paranoia and mistrust in the ones around us.

People that have self-love are mindful of who they are, rather than dwelling on what others think. They are conscious about what they need versus just what they want. They stay focused on things that will push them closer to their goals of moving forward in life. When we love ourselves, we take better care of our hygiene, nutrition, exercise, we get proper sleep, and have better social interactions. Self-love helps us to understand when "No means no." We don't take part in relationships that will harm us physically, socially, emotionally, or spiritually. We learn how to set boundaries effectively.

When we have self-love, we learn discernment. We know the ones who are truly rooting for us and don't take pleasure in our pain. The haters will hate, and we don't have to entertain their negativity. Self-love causes us to love ourselves and make healthy choices for our lives. We cherish spending quality time alone and we enjoy taking ourselves to a dinner and a movie.

Why are we our worst critics? As humans we can be so hard on ourselves. We must accept our humanness and understand that we are not perfect. We will forgive someone else at the blink of an eye, but it takes years for us to forgive ourselves. Life is about making mistakes. Learn from your bad habits, change your ways and stop it completely. When we live intentionally for God, he will bless us with purpose and design in his own timing. Lighten up on yourself and live your best life.

Flower Girl

She is a flower
But she doesn't know it
The sun is shining on her
But she still hasn't grown yet
She's deeply rooted
Just waiting to sprout
She was watered by the rain
We're ready for her to blossom out
Oh, what a beautiful flower she'll be
Standing tall for everyone to see
For she's more than just looks
There's something about her, can't you tell
This flower isn't meant to be bought
Oh no, she's not for sale
Her purpose was simple
To prove it could be done
Now the garden is full of beautiful flowers
Standing tall each and every one

Chapter Seven

TEACHERS ARE OUR HEROES

I absolutely love being a teacher! It is so rewarding to see your hard work paying off when a student makes a good grade, accomplish a goal that they've struggled with, or seeing a student making new friends. I treat my students like they are my own children. I am overprotective of them because if someone puts their hands on them in any way, I will end up like Samuel L. Jackson in "A Time to Kill!" All jokes aside, teachers give children purpose, they help them become successful citizens in the world and inspire them to be the very best in life.

Teachers are heroes because of the dedication and perseverance in making teaching and learning possible for all children. They give of themselves, they wear many hats, always going extra lengths to reach every child.

During the pandemic, teachers not only focused on making sure their students were learning, whether it was face to face or virtual, they also made sure that their psychological needs were met. COVID-19 played a huge role on the mental state of the students and their families, and the teachers were there for support.

Teachers build a positive classroom environment, they help students deal with stress in their daily lives, they make learning and reading fun, empathize when students are emotional, help them build friendships, and always encourage their students to be lifelong learners.

I remember when I attended Baptist Hill Kindergarten, I was on the playground standing alone watching the other students play together. They were playing fun games and getting on the playground equipment that I loved. I was very shy and didn't know how to make friends. The teachers were in a group laughing and sharing stories with each other. For some reason, I never felt accepted when I was away from home. I often stayed to myself because I felt I didn't measure up to the other children.

Out of the blue, a teacher came over and gave me a gentle hug and rubbed my hair and told me that I was a very pretty little girl. She spoke so sweet and softly to me. She nudged me and told me that it was ok to go and play and make new friends. I felt so special. It was amazing how that little gesture gave me all the confidence in the world. She wasn't even my teacher; it was like she was an angel that suddenly appeared. Without hesitation I ran on the playground and from that day forward I was never alone at recess.

The teacher that helped me to build up my confidence in kindergarten, and currently serves as a mentor for me today is Mrs. Gloria C. Warren. For over 30 years, her and her husband Mr. George Warren has inspired and impacted the lives of students at W. O. Parmer Elementary School in Greenville, Alabama and the community. Mrs. Warren is not only a mentor to me but also my pastor. Her and her husband's ministry is very uplifting and provides Godly principles for women and men.

As a leading lady, Pastor Warren displays her resilience and a relatable transparency in her ministry which is why many flock to hear her preach the word of God. Her messages give us a beckon of hope to know that brighter days are ahead. Her son Girard is my classmate, the Class of 1999 and Founder of the All Class Reunion held in Greenville during Memorial Day weekend. It is an annual event where graduates of Greenville High School, friends and family enjoy food, fun, and fellowship. It is a perfect way to network and rekindle old friendships. This event is so amazing and a sight to see. Attendees enjoy a weekend of fun activities with their classmates in a spacious lot in the city with every class representing under their own tents enjoying barbecues, crawfish boils, fish fry's, games, music and more.

Local radio stations enjoy the fun as the crowd is hyped by the latest jams, prize giveaways, dance contests and line dancing. Every class is represented with personalized class reunion T-shirts and some even had theme styled gatherings. Graduating classes as early as 1971 all the way to 2019 have attended. The social experience is wonderful as you get a chance to visit with other classes. It was funny to see the Class of 1980, when they were graduating high school, I was just being born. On Saturday nights many classes enjoy hanging out at a lounge, going to a movie, restaurants, house parties, or dances at the local recreation center. Some class reunions even enjoyed Sunday service together, engaging in praise and worship and partaking in the Holy Communion. The weekend is filled with so many activities that there is very little time to sleep.

Pastor Warren and her family have been involved in many community efforts that no one ever knew about. On any given day you may find her, her husband, sons and granddaughters picking up trash along city streets and many other areas in the community. How do I know? I have been there with them picking up trash. The Warrens give a true meaning of servant leaders. Pastor Warren was raised in a family of givers and had a love for teaching at an early age because her Mom was a second grade teacher. The Cook family loved ministering and helping others.

Pastor Warren and her sisters started giving back to the community many years ago, hosting holiday events and enjoying catering Thanksgiving on the Hill. This event is held on Thanksgiving Day in Greenville, where they provide hot catered meals to the community. What makes it truly beautiful is that they don't do it for publicity. They love spreading kindness to others because it truly brings them joy to see the smiling faces and know that they have blessed many families.

Not only do I admire the love they have for the community and seeing children learning and growing, but I also admire their marriage. It is amazing how well the Warrens seem to be so perfect for each other, and because they have been married and working together for so long, it is like they are joined at the hip. I love how they constantly complete each other's sentences. I know there are no perfect marriages, but I love the chemistry they have with each other. A happy marriage brings joy and glory to God.

Michelle Obama says, "Marriage is a choice you make every day. You don't do it because it's easy. You do it because you believe in it. You believe in the other person. Marry your equal, someone who wants you to win as much as you want them to win."

Chapter Eight

WHEREFORE ART THOU MY HUSBAND?

I believe that having a loving, God-fearing spouse is the best gift of all. I know a successful marriage is not finding the right mate, but also being the right mate. God is still working on me and there's some things I would like to improve within myself before God will bless me with a husband. I often pray that when the timing is right, God will send me my happily ever after. While we may not like being single, God needs our attention in this season. Let him mold, develop, and prepare us before he gives us to someone.

Sometimes we got to let go of the attachment but keep the lesson. When God blesses me to be married, I would like for it to be forever. So many marriages end in divorce when trials arise, but I want our marriage to last forever. I would like for me and my significant other to fight to stay together and not give up when life gets tough.

I pray that God blesses me with not just what I want, but what I need. My husband will have a close relationship with God and his family. I want to be at peace knowing that God will be in the center of our marriage. I want him to be a praying husband and I will be a praying wife. I'm looking for someone with emotional maturity. Everyone may come with flaws, but I don't want them to allow their emotions to rule their actions.

I am looking for someone who is open-minded, have a willingness to communicate effectively and give feedback. I want to be best friends with my spouse. I would like to build a solid foundation together. Some women claim they don't need a man to be happy. They are independent and can do bad all by themselves. I don't need to watch too much reality TV and eat fast food, but I do, I don't need it, but like a good man, it will make my life more enjoyable. Saying things like *I don't need a man* may be a way single women can downplay those that are happily married, it gives them a sense of empowerment. It is important to always be happy for others, because everyone has their own path to follow.

Nowadays, women aren't waiting on a husband to bare children. If women want children, they have the options of getting a sperm donor, adopting or fostering children. Education plays a huge part in women being more self-sufficient and marriage is seen as only an option not a necessity. I love to see independent women following their dreams and having options, but I will never cancel having a lifelong companion, even if I can stand on my own two feet. I do feel that we should strive to make ourselves happy first, but honestly, I want that special someone to keep me warm at night. I love seeing couples that are happily married because it inspires me to know that one day God will bless me.

Women endure a lot in relationships and saying, *I don't need a man*, may be a coping mechanism because they are tired of getting hurt. You cannot judge an entire gender for a few bad relationships. I understand that going through a terrible breakup can make a woman or man bitter and angry to the point where he or she doesn't want to re-visit the hurt again. I have been in relationships where it didn't go as planned but it wasn't entirely the man's fault, it takes two. Society has made it cool to put down men, just because they are men, and that is wrong.

We may have plenty of education, houses, cars, traveled to many places, but it doesn't take the place of a lifetime companion. Who really wants to grow old alone? Some don't want to be bothered with their own man but will jump at the opportunity to be with someone else's husband. I know about this firsthand, so much that I have included it in my book. I have done some things that wasn't pleasing to God as well. I have made bad decisions, but thankfully I have learned from them, and it has helped me become the woman I am today. Dating someone that is in another relationship is not healthy and will end with someone eventually getting hurt. You won't be able to trust them, it is very risky, damaging to your own self-esteem and truly painful. I believe we can enjoy being single, but it doesn't mean we can't open our heart to love.

When God blesses you with the right partner you will have social and emotional support which will help you tackle the stresses of life better. Being in a happy and healthy relationship is linked to a longer lifespan, it promotes bonding and comfort and helps your overall mood. The burdens of life can weigh heavily on an individual. Having a partner to vent to and help you get through the tough times can be rewarding. The key is to allow God to pick the right companion for you.

Many times, we don't have successful relationships because we are doing things on our own and not consulting with God first. We are enticed by the type of car they drive, where they live, the money they make, the way they look, or the family they were brought up in. These things matter but shouldn't be our top priorities. Love, commitment, honesty and understanding allows us to know if our partner truly cares about us, is coming from a good place, and supports us. Showing love, respect, and kindness in our relationship will keep everyone happy.

When we focus on bringing happiness to the relationship, we feel more secure and content in our life. It takes hard work and sacrifices to maintain a strong relationship. Knowing how to communicate with your partner is key. Spending quality time, showing love and affection, establishing boundaries, respect and working together helps in building a strong foundation for the both of us. These are the things I pray to God for daily. I have never been married but I pay close attention to successful marriages around me. Each person plays an important role in the relationship, and it takes a lot of hard work and dedication to be married and to stay happily married.

Sometimes men aren't the best communicators, and it will create discourse in the relationship. Honest communication is essential to any relationship. Women should take the time to listen because some men may communicate what their expectations are, but as women sometimes we hear what we want to hear. They may tell us that they are not looking for a serious relationship but something casual. We continue to try to change his mind.

They may tell us upfront that they only want to have sex, but we are trying our best to force them down the aisle. They express to us that they don't want to have children, but we stop taking our birth control pills because we want to trap them into fatherhood. Although he should have protected himself and worn a condom, we were warned upfront but decided not to listen.

Although it takes two to tango, we can't get mad if they aren't supportive in our child's life. It will be unfortunate for the child not to be able to experience the love from both parents, because we have attempted to pressure him into something that he is not ready for. This type of behavior will set us up to have a disastrous relationship.

Men should always align their words with their actions. Honesty is a huge one for me. I am too old to be playing games, always wondering if my spouse is being truthful. The more expressive a man is with his feelings the more genuine he will be as a partner. Understanding your partner's wants and desires is essential in having a healthy relationship. Take the time to listen. Be supportive in every aspect, whether it is wins or losses, support is needed. In a relationship both partners should always strive to refine their character to achieve the lasting love that you both deserve.

Dating can be frustrating especially when we meet someone, and we connect so well and think they are "The One." We invest a lot of time, emotions and energy into the relationship, and it doesn't work out. We must pay close attention at the beginning, because we may see signs that the relationship will lead to bliss or misery. It is hard but we can't make excuses for their bad behavior because we are tired of dating and our biological clock is ticking. It will be us having to deal with an unhappy life.

Marriage is a goal for me. The true picture for marriage is that it symbolizes the love of Christ for us. God's desires are that we be made more into the image of Him. God's plans for marriage are a covenant relationship, where everything is centered in Christ. This is what will carry us through the good and bad times.

One day we'll meet a guy and ultimately, he's going to find out how we chew, how sensitive we are, how we dance, how our face looks underneath our makeup (I don't really wear any), how we can be hyper at times, cranky when we are tired, how we think we look fat in every photo, and how bad our breath is in the morning. He will know EVERYTHING about us, and you know what? He is still going to love us. That's the kind of love I am praying for.

Real Love

It's easy to say I love you
But do you really mean it
Should I believe you because you said it?
I want to be able to love with my whole heart, not just let someone rent it
If you love me, you have to show me
When you look at me if it's love, then tell me what you see
Do you see that I have more gray on the left side of my head?
Nah, you missed that because you were thinking about getting me into your bed
Did you notice how country I sound when I talk?
No, you were too busy watching my behind as I walked
Do you know I get excited when I see others win?
Nope, you were scared to lose the fun with me, you wanted me to sin
If you love me don't just say it, prove it to me
Love everything about me, even what the eyes can't see

I want someone that actions meet their words and are open about how they feel. Respect is another quality I look for. I want us to encourage each other and appreciate the things that we may be passionate about. When there are disagreements, it is ok to agree to disagree, but still respect each other's differences. Having a sense of independence is great for the marriage because although two will become one, you don't want to lose who you are.

Even married you can still maintain your individuality, enjoying some separate activities, but have interest that you may share with your spouse. I would love to learn new things and have new friendships together, always keeping the romance and love alive. I want me and my love to enjoy good conversations, weekend getaways, binge watching our favorite shows, intimate dinners, a walk in the park, praying together, hugs and kisses and crazy, spontaneous sex. I deserve to get pleasure from my husband and not feel guilty.

I want him to understand that sometimes I can be a wild sleeper. When I first fall asleep my body is positioned vertical, later it changes to horizontal, but when I wake up, I am upside down. Throughout the night I probably have made every shape imaginable. I'm ready to embark on the not so fun things like paying bills together, disagreements, occasional silent treatments, going through grief, taking care of each other when someone is not feeling well and just everyday living. I truly want to grow old with the one I love. Empathy is also important in a relationship because I want to know that my partner understands my struggles and aim to help me by showing me compassion.

Although appearance is not the most important to me, I would like someone that I am physically attracted to, and he is to me. Relationships need love, affection, and acknowledgement. I want us to be attracted to each other and not be afraid to express it verbally and physically. Last but not least, I want my husband to be funny. I love to entertain my social media followers by posting jokes of the day or something inspirational. Just the other day I posted, "Your mind is like your bed, you have to make it up every day and be careful who you let in it. At my funeral sit me up, I want to see who is rubbing my husband's back, asking if everything is ok."

Laughter is the best medicine especially in a relationship. I love to laugh and love making others laugh. Have you ever thought about things that make you go hmmm?

If the #2 pencil is so popular, then why is it considered #2? What hair color would they put on the driver's licenses of bald men? Why do hotdogs come ten to a package, but the hot dog buns only have eight? How would we know if a word in the dictionary is misspelled? If Barbie is so popular, then why do we have to buy her friends? If the police officer arrests a mime, do they tell him he has the right to remain silent? Does Lipton employees usually take coffee breaks? Okay…okay last one, why do they put Braille on the drive through ATM bank machines? I don't know the answers, just giving us something to take our minds off the issues that we're going through.

Take the time to live, love and laugh. God got us and our situation. Okay! So, stop worrying and have faith. Life is not meant to be serious all the time. I don't have a man yet, but I am not worrying because God knows what I desire. I want someone easy going, where I can be free to be me. Someone who is fun, honest, positive and happy, and don't sweat the small stuff. I am a good woman, and I will wait patiently for God to send me a good man.

Hands down! I'm the "Best Catch of the Year!" I'm an educator, and I have never been married. I have three grown children, an amazing son with autism, and two wonderful daughters. I am super smart, super funny, super cute and super sexy. Let's grow old together! I have always been attracted to men with a great personality, funny, tall, good-looking seasoned men. As long as you and your teeth sleep together, WE ARE GOOD!

I have a great personality with a good sense of humor. I'm tall, I have legs longer than some people's dreams. I love that I can grab things off the top shelf. If we become a couple, being with me, you will never be hungry because I can cook some amazing noodles. The last time I was someone's match I was donating blood. I'm everything your mother ever wanted for you. I possess a lot of great qualities, I'm a smart and talented cookie with a smile that will leave you mesmerized with my beauty, and if you have always wanted to read your woman like a book, now is your chance. I pray God blesses me with at least 60 more years of health and happiness.

Laughter is Good for the Soul

Laughter is my medicine, it takes the pain away
The pain from my heart, my life, the pain in the world today
When I see someone sad, I just want to make them smile
I need it myself, every once in a while
I'm not a comedian by any means
But laughing is how I've learned to deal with things
Whatever it takes to brighten someone's day
We laugh and we talk all those feelings away

Chapter Nine

FORGIVENESS IN THE EYES OF GOD

Writing has really helped me tremendously to express my emotions and put things in perspective. I am a sinner and haven't always treated people with love and kindness. I know I could be a better person if I wasn't engulfed in feelings of bitterness, defeat, and solitude. Do you struggle with forgiveness? I am convinced that if I keep writing about forgiveness then I will take a leap of faith to forgive myself and others.

I am definitely not a holy roller, but I do believe in God's word. **Ephesians 4:32**, states "Be kind and compassionate to one another, forgiving each other, just as in Christ God forgave you." **Matthew 6:14**, "For if you forgive other people when they sin against you, your heavenly Father will also forgive you." **Colossians 3:13**, "Bear with each other and forgive one another if any of you has a grievance against someone. Forgive as the Lord forgave you." **Luke 6:37**, "Do not judge, and you will not be judged. Do not condemn, and you will not be condemned. Forgive, and you will be forgiven." **Psalms 32:1**, "Blessed is the one whose transgressions are forgiven, whose sins are covered."

Proverbs 17:9, "Love prospers when a fault is forgiven, but dwelling on it separates close friends." **1 John 1:9**, "If we confess our sins, he is faithful and just to forgive us our sins and to cleanse us from all unrighteousness." I hope this may help someone that is struggling with forgiveness. Forgiveness is a gift that we give ourselves. It is not for the other person but for us to move on with our lives so that God may make room for us to receive more blessings. Although I understand this concept, he is still working on me. I like to say, forgive the ones that cause us pain because our soul deserves peace.

I recall attending a church service one night when surprisingly my uncle, who is an active member of his church got up before the congregation to do a short talk. What was shocking was that he was talking to the entire congregation, asking for forgiveness. He expressed if he had done anything wrong to anyone, he would like to say he was sorry. I never looked up keeping my head down because it wasn't an apology to me personally. It seemed like he was trying to clear his own conscience of his wrongdoings.

That memory played in my head repeatedly for years. If he sincerely wanted to apologize to me, it should have been face to face. Although I only told my Mom what my uncle did to me, I felt that other family members knew but kept quiet. I thank God so much for my Aunt Naomi who always checked to see how I was doing and helped me seek help. The only way I was comfortable trying to cope with being raped was to stay away from my family and most of all my uncle.

I know we are imperfect beings, and we all make mistakes. After a lot of soul searching, I realized that forgiveness is about letting go and preventing the person's behavior from destroying your heart. I don't want to be bitter but better in love, happiness, and forgiveness. God, please release me out of bondage! I want to be free! Free! Free! I honestly will admit that God is still working on me in the area of forgiveness. I continue to take it one day at a time. I pray that God heals me and heals my heart to forgive others as he has forgiven me.

Chapter Ten

HELP A FRIEND IN NEED

I am very grateful to meet my best friend Megan when I joined AmeriCorps. AmeriCorps is a program that places thousands of people into intensive service positions, where they learn valuable skills, earn money for education, and develop a strong sense of civic responsibility. They serve members by creating jobs and providing pathways to opportunity as they enter the workforce.

When Megan and I met it was an instant connection, it was like we had known each other forever. She is my best friend but more like a sister to me. Although we are around five years apart it felt like we were just destined to be besties. Megan and I are members of an empowerment group of ladies that was handpicked by Prophetess Lillian, who's her aunt. Many people face daily challenges and don't have any support, but this group is great for sharing inspirational talks to help uplift others without judgement.

When Megan came to visit and Jaycen got aggressive, she would immediately jump in to help restrain him. She looked at Jaycen as her own son, she never seemed to get tired of helping me and the girls. Megan and I had so much in common, we would laugh and cry together, we are best friends for life! Megan is my #1 cheerleader. She is more like family than a friend. I am happy that God blessed me with a wonderful best friend.

There were so many incidents where Megan stood in the midst of Jaycen's tantrums. One weekend we decided to take a trip and do some shopping. Megan was driving and he and the girls were sitting in the back seat. Jaycen was sitting directly behind Megan. He started becoming very irritated and began kicking Megan's seat while she was driving.

I pleaded and begged Jaycen to stop kicking her seat, but the more I asked the worse he got. "Jaycen please stop!!" "Please Jaycen!!" I yelled. "We can have an accident and get hurt," I tried to explain to him. The girls very calmly asked him to stop but he continued to kick the seat as hard as he could.

Megan did not stop the car, she kept driving and acted just like it didn't bother her. That day I officially knew that she was my ride or die friend. She was humiliated by Jaycen but because of the love she had for me and my family, she kept her cool. When we started to ignore Jaycen and his ranting, he stopped kicking her seat. There was nothing off limits when talking to Megan. She knew my whole life story and I knew hers. Megan knows everything about me, and I trust her wholeheartedly. Sometimes it wasn't much for her to say, but just being there and listening was truly all I needed.

When someone is going through a storm, your silent presence is more powerful than a million empty words. Megan helped me to vent when I wasn't having a good day. When she grieved her fiancé's death I was there for her. We were always there for each other. She knew that I had low self-esteem and would always uplift me. I could talk openly to her about being raped as a child and not having the support from my family. She understood my struggle with forgiveness and always encouraged me. When I am sad, Megan was always there to make sure I'm okay. I'm so thankful to God that he placed us along the same path.

My Ride or Die Chick

She's my friend but not just that
She is my peace
My balance
My calm in the storm
My sun when it's raining
My understanding when I'm confused
My listening ear when I have something to say
My light in the darkness
She picks me up when I have fallen
She tells me it's going to be ok
She reassures me when I have doubt
She makes me laugh when I want to cry
She redirects me when I'm off track
She's not just my friend, she's more than that
She's my SISTAR

If you are the friend of a sexually abused survivor, it is very hard to know what to say. It is very important to remember to remain calm and empathetic, always striving to be supportive and nonjudgmental, and assure them that you believe them. It is hard to see a friend in pain and agony but try not to make threats against the perpetrator, because it will only add more stress to the situation.

Lastly, as a true friend keep this information confidential, because it is not your story to tell. Don't be afraid to assist them in getting a medical exam done and contacting the appropriate authorities. I know that I would be a better person if I would have had the support from my family. I would be able to heal and forgive a lot quicker.

I am praying that one-day God places it on my heart to forgive. "I Need Thee!" I keep telling myself repeatedly. Forgiveness is a very powerful weapon; it is not just for you but the other person. Having forgiveness in your heart is showing love. It doesn't mean you are giving the wrongdoer a pass of approval; it is basically saying you are rising above the situation and moving forward. I'm human and I struggle with this daily. I am so thankful for my best friend who constantly helps me. Each day is a new opportunity to get it right. It is never too late, because God's timing is the best timing and I'm truly working on letting go and letting God.

Chapter Eleven

UNPLANNED PARENTHOOD

We all may have deep-seated wounds from our past that shape us in very profound ways. I was 14 years old when I found out that I was pregnant with my son, and I felt lonely and afraid. I was only a child, still playing with dolls. I had a make-believe friend, but I was about to have a baby, a whole human being. I was preparing to be responsible for another life and I didn't even have a life of my own yet. I didn't care about no one's reaction except my Grandmothers.

I remember being so afraid to tell her that I was pregnant. Finally, one day I got up the courage and I told her, her response was a breath of fresh air. I remember her saying, "Jacquie you are not the first and won't be the last teenager to become pregnant." I loved her even more for showing me unconditional love and not judging me.

Of course, she was not condoning teenage pregnancy, because honestly speaking, it is the hardest journey when you are responsible for another life, and you are struggling and still learning and growing into maturity. I was faced with a lot of criticism from my family, but mainly from my own thinking. What kind of mother would I be?

How can I love another individual when I really didn't love myself? I was about to bring a beautiful, precious, innocent and untainted baby into the world. While pregnant I felt that everyone was staring and whispering about the young, naïve, teenager that had nothing.

As my belly grew, I felt humiliated and ashamed. I couldn't wait until after the baby was born so I could return to some form of normalcy. I decided to quit school in the 10th grade. My family wasn't happy, but it was the best decision for me at the time. I promised myself that I would not allow this pregnancy to defeat me in furthering my education, it would only be a slight delay.

Although, I had to take an alternative route to receive my high school diploma, through my hard work and determination, I was still able to graduate the same year as my classmates in 1999. I didn't get a chance to experience the baby showers and gender reveals like today's popular events that occur before your baby is born.

I was very grateful that although it wasn't an ideal situation, my Mom bought everything I needed for her first grandchild. I was very thankful for the love and support she provided for my son. Her many sacrifices were greatly appreciated. Jaycen was the only baby in the house, and he was truly spoiled by everyone.

My oldest brother Jacob worked at Piggly Wiggly supermarket in high school and every week he was spending most of his paycheck on clothes, pampers and formula for his nephew Jaycen. I was so thankful for the help I got from my family. After my son was born, I felt a great deal of relief and things got better but the burden of being a teenage mother came with consequences.

One day I was walking to the neighborhood grocery store with Jaycen. We loved supporting black owned businesses, it was a community favorite. They had everything imaginable, and I loved that it was in walking distance. The Johnsons were the owners, and they were members of my church. We looked forward to buying items and having a good time laughing and getting a word of encouragement.

The journey walking there every week included me and Jaycen getting a lot of stares. Jaycen was tall and skinny, and at only three years old he appeared to be around six because he was very tall for his age. I remember cars would slow down and the passengers would stare at us as they passed by. I carried Jaycen on my hip and his feet would be dragging on the ground. I'm sure it was a sight to see, but no one really knew my situation and if they did, no one extended a helping hand.

Many years of carrying Jaycen on my hip has put an indention on my right hip bone but holding him was the only way I knew how to protect him. Jaycen could walk but he wasn't a very good walker, and I often feared if I put him down, he was so strong he would run away from me. I would be so tired from the walk to the store that Jaycen and I would often stay indoors because having to struggle with him every day was truly a chore. I love my son, but I wouldn't wish being a single teenage parent on no one because not only do you struggle, but you also find yourself in very tough situations and you don't know which way to turn.

Like me, the prevalence of births to teenage mothers negatively affects high school graduation and increases unemployment. Without a high school diploma or equivalent, teenagers and adults may have greater difficulty securing quality employment and have lower earning potential. It is hard to show your capability if you don't have the education or skillset to back it up. A less educated population and unskilled workforce negatively affects the economy and makes it difficult for communities to break aggressive cycles of poverty and crime.

When a baby is born to a teenage mother, he or she is likely to have more difficulty acquiring cognitive and language skills, as well as social and emotional skills like self-control, self-esteem and self-confidence. Sometimes the teenager is still developing into their own self-image. Most of the time, like me, a teen Mom is clueless about rearing a child.

Some teenage mothers are often more aggressive with their children, because they don't know how to communicate effectively, and they tend to blame their child for not being able to fully enjoy their teenage years. However, some will step up to the plate, take ownership, and make the best of the situation by being responsible and providing for their child's well-being. What helped me to prosper was because I wanted better for me and my child, and I was encouraged by the naysayers, the ones that sat back and watched waiting on me to fail.

Negativity can sometimes motivate people to do better, it gives them the challenge to continue to pursue their goals. As their child gets older some teenage mothers may abandon their own aspirations in an effort to ensure that academic and career goals are attainable for their child.

What can be done to stop these cycles of teenage pregnancy? Sex education programs that teach the benefits of abstinence and pregnancy prevention are essential. Parents, mentors and educators can share in this responsibility by ensuring that teens gain this knowledge at home and at school.

Avoiding discussions on the issue of sex and safe practices only heightens potential for teen pregnancy to occur. Talk with your children about the negative effects of sex. They may or may not listen, but at least you have provided them with some guidance. There isn't a specific age to have these conversations. When your child starts to inquire, you can have an open discussion so that they are given accurate information from an adult. Although it may be uncomfortable, if it is a two-parent home, getting the perspective from Mom and Dad is necessary.

Not only can you get pregnant, but there are also multiple diseases related to having unprotected sex. Many people think there are only two STD's, syphilis and gonorrhea. There is also HIV, (the virus that causes AIDS), vaginitis, herpes, chlamydia, genital warts, and many others. Some of the best ways to not get infected is to abstain from sex, stay with one uninfected partner, use condoms consistently and correctly, and communicate effectively with your partner.

If you are unmarried, you should definitely wait until God sends you your husband or wife. Be smart about the decisions that you make because if it is not thought out properly, it could lead to a lifetime of health issues and death.

When my son Jaycen was born I didn't know much about babies. I had only babysat a few times, but I noticed everything he was doing was so much slower than the other babies I had been around. It took him forever to sit up and crawl. He was a little over two years old before he ever started walking. If that wasn't alarming enough, when he cried sometimes, he would hold his breath, just for a few seconds, but I knew something wasn't right.

We spent a lot of time in early intervention programs and eventually my son was diagnosed with autism at the age of two. As my son got older, we noticed that he couldn't communicate with us and we couldn't understand him, which truly made it a rough couple of years. We all struggled because this was something different. I didn't know what autism was, I had never heard of it, and I was scared. It's weird how things worked out. Jaycen had to have tubes put in his ears. My family and I developed our own way of communicating with him and it worked for us.

I am so blessed to have my siblings in my life. If it wasn't for my oldest brother Jacob, I don't know how I would have made it when Jaycen was a baby. He stepped in effortlessly to assist me where he saw help was needed. What I absolutely loved about Jacob is that he didn't have to get praise or recognition for being a loving and caring big brother.

I am so proud of the man he has become. Jacob served in the United States Marine Corps and is now a 20-year retired veteran residing in South Carolina. Growing up my second oldest brother Joel and I were very close. Both of us shared the same Mom and Dad and have a deep passion for helping others. Joel was more than just an uncle, he was like a Dad to my girls because he helped me out a lot with them.

Joel continuously supports me by hosting Autism Awareness benefit programs in Columbus, Georgia in honor of my son Jaycen. Our family and friends were so happy when my brother was surprisingly honored for always giving back. Joel loves to volunteer, and was surprised on his birthday, November 16, 2021 with a proclamation for his volunteerism. The City of Columbus honored him with his own day! Joel is very well known in the Columbus area and has won numerous awards for his work in the community. He has a non-profit organization called "Books and Bookshelves in Barbershops," promoting literacy amongst the youth. He also enjoys volunteering in the reading programs with the Columbus City School System and so much more. I am very proud of the accomplishments of both of my handsome brothers. Our grandparents instilled in us as children of the importance of helping others. They are truly smiling down on us.

Julia is our beautiful baby sister, and she is truly spoiled rotten. Julia and I have totally different personalities. Whatever Julia wants, Julia gets. I'll admit, I am part of the reason she is so spoiled, but I guess that's part of being a big sister. Julia shocked us all at 18, she was pregnant, and no one knew it. Family support means everything. I am so grateful that I was able to name my nephew and cut the umbilical cord. I love my baby sister; she is a wonderful mother. Julia is happily married and living in Wetumpka, Alabama, raising my smart, strong and handsome 16-year-old nephew. I love being Auntie Jacquie to all my nieces and nephews.

JUST J'S, MY 3

Chapter Twelve

AUTISM STRONG MOM

Autism is a serious developmental disorder that impairs the ability to communicate and interact effectively. Some of the symptoms of Autism can vary but in the case of my son, he was non-verbal, so he constantly had difficulty with communication, social interaction, compulsive and aggressive behaviors, displayed physical abuse to others, learning disabilities, unaware of other's emotions and sensitivity to sounds.

I literally cried every day because I didn't fully understand his illnesses and sometimes, I felt like a failure. Autism doesn't come with a manual, just a Mom, and I was afraid of my child, but I knew if I could get him in the right treatment program it would help him, me and my girls.

As a baby I wouldn't allow Jaycen to do much for himself. I catered to his every need because I knew that he would grow up differently. In my mind, I thought I was helping him from not suffering. He was my beautiful baby boy and although he was different, he was mine and I was going to make sure that he had everything that he wanted.

What I didn't realize was that I was doing more harm to him than good. It was like I delayed him even more because I wouldn't allow him to try to do things for himself. I was saddened that my son wouldn't have a normal life that I had hoped for. I had to educate myself about his illnesses to understand how to deal with his behaviors.

Autism disorders is a lifelong developmental disability that can limit social, educational, occupational and other important demands in every stage of your life. Jaycen attended an early intervention program where he started speech and occupational therapy. He was all our priority and as the only baby we had in the house, he was definitely spoiled by everyone.

Although females can be autistic, it is very prevalent in first born male children. Not only does their symptoms of autism affect the child, but the whole family. I love my son dearly but having to care for him stressed me mentally, physically, and emotionally.

Parental stress is so real, especially when you have an autistic child that behavior is often elevated. I constantly felt a loss of personal control with the absence of his Dad and lack of professional support. Jaycen was very challenging to deal with especially when he was exposed to sensitive sounds.

For instance, he despised the TV. It was nothing for him to go through our house punching our 32″ and 55″ TV's. He had broken so many of them that my girls and I didn't know what was going on in the world. When I got to work my co-workers would tell me about some of my favorite reality shows and what was happening in the news. We were without a television for more than a year.

I love my son Jaycen but it was truly hard dealing with him. He was often very violent towards me, and my girls and I felt that I had very little support. Jaycen would fight with me so much that over a period he gave me two black eyes. Yes, I got beat up by my own autistic son. I hadn't ever had a man to beat me, but my son did. My daughters often came to my rescue, but I was afraid that they would get hurt.

Fighting with Jaycen was so exhausting. It was like I was in a boxing match, often having the taste of blood and sweat on my tongue. It was so hurtful, the thought of your own flesh and blood, first born child slapping, punching, pushing, and biting you, but I kept reminding myself of his illness.

I often asked God why I would be given this type of life. I kept feeling unloved and unwanted by my family and God. It was nothing for Jaycen to disrespect his Grandma and slap her glasses off her face. Before Jaycen was born I had never heard of autism. Jaycen's violent behavior towards me and the girls was so intense it made me wonder if I was being punished by God. I didn't know anyone with the illness, I felt alone in my journey. I needed a support group, someone to educate me on his illnesses and symptoms. Autism is a part of my child, but it is not everything he is. He is so much more than his diagnosis. I love Jaycen and my girls more than I could ever love myself.

Chapter Thirteen

PARENTAL and SOCIETAL REJECTIONS

When Jaycen was younger I knew he needed a father figure in his life. Although my brothers were a great support for me and my children, I needed more. I remember I got the courage to introduce him to his biological father when he was two years old. I told him that I needed help with our son, and I wanted him to be in his life, even if we weren't going to be a couple. He hurt me so bad that day, saying, "Jaycen is not my son, because I don't make retarded babies."

Jaycen was a handful, but when it comes to my boy that I pushed out, I'm never going to sit down and shut up! I will say and do everything that he can't. I hated him for rejecting his son, but after that conversation we never spoke again. It was hard being a teenage mother, but especially hard when you have a special needs child.

On top of the rejection, it was very difficult for me to find a daycare to take care of Jaycen while I looked for a job. When a facility rejects your child, it is hard not to take it personal. My Mom asked my cousins Annie Jewel and Shirley Ann Williams, who had an in-home daycare in the Mount Zion community where we lived if they could watch him. I was so happy they agreed to keep him and my Mom would pick him up after she got off work, because it was on her route. They told us to bring Jaycen and they would take good care of him. They did just that! Every evening when my Mom would pick my baby up, he was so happy, always smelling good with a shiny face full of Vaseline and a full stomach.

Cousin Jewel called everybody in the community family, and she truly took care of everyone and their children. Jaycen looked forward to going to their daycare and even though he faced a lot of challenges, they didn't treat him any different than the rest of the children. They loved him so much, they called him their "wee one."

Cousin Jewel was known for her home cooked soul food and fruit cakes that she sold during Christmas. When you opened her front door you could smell the aroma of collard greens, hot water cornbread, fried chicken, macaroni and cheese, and fried corn. During the holidays she would have her sweet potato pies, egg pies, caramel cakes, pound cakes, and chocolate cakes lined up on the deep freezer to cool. Sometimes she would even make me and Jaycen a plate for our dinner, which was such a relief after a hard day at work.

My cousins loved taking care of children, all the neighborhood families loved them. They provided the children with good food, love and kindness, and some discipline when needed. It is very hard to say goodbye to our loved ones. Our beloved caretakers are no longer with us today. The memories of them will last for a lifetime. I pray that they both continue to rest in heavenly peace.

As Jaycen got older he became more aggressive and had to attend a learning center for older children. It was hard to deal with Jaycen in public places. I remember one weekend I was struggling with him coming out of a store. No one tried to help me, I only got blank stares. Jaycen was about twelve years old, it was so humiliating because I could see people turning their heads when I made eye contact. I could hear the whispers, and I truly hated how people responded to children with autism or children that were different. I didn't know how to deal with it, and there was no professional organization to help with assistance besides the police department.

The Greenville Police Department knew me on a first name basis because I had called so many times. Usually, the conversation began with Jaycen has run away again, can you please help me find him? Another question might be, Jaycen is fighting us, could you get someone to help restrain him?

There were so many days that I stayed on the phone calling around to see who would accept my son into their treatment program. As Jaycen got older and older it got even harder to find somewhere for him to go. When I mentioned to them that my son had autism, I was immediately turned away because they would say that they didn't have anyone licensed to work with autistic children. After many years of no success over the phone and a lot of rejections, my girls and I started driving all over the state of Alabama. We traveled to Opelika, Dothan, Mobile, Tallassee, Birmingham and Montgomery.

I finally got a call from a residential facility in Tallassee and Mobile but since Tallassee was closer to me, I chose that location. When Jaycen was 17, I enrolled him into a behavioral residential facility for adolescence in Tallassee. This is when I witnessed that he could do things like tying his shoes and feeding himself. They had taught him these new skills in a matter of a few weeks. I was doing mostly all of this for him at home.

I was so thankful that he was placed on the right medication, and it was uphill from there. It is very important that you give positive reinforcement when dealing with children with autism, always rewarding good behavior, praising them when they have good manners or learn a new skill. His behavior started to get better because he was happy to be around other children his age that he could learn from.

After Jaycen turned 21, he was transferred to a facility in Montgomery. He loves it there and I am happy that he is not that far away from home. I have seen so much growth in Jaycen since relocating to Montgomery. I am so happy that my son is thriving! Looking back over the years, the struggle was so real trying to find a treatment program. It had become very humiliating and exhausting for me, the girls and Jaycen who loved to act out while riding in the car, not to mention the high gas expenses while traveling the state.

When Jaycen was younger, I remember us taking a trip over the weekend to visit my cousins in Birmingham. It was a fun weekend of pampering ourselves as we went to the hair salon to get our hair braided. As mothers we always put our children first, but this weekend while visiting my cousins, I was happy to treat myself. On our way back home to Greenville, which is a 2-hour drive, while I was driving, Jaycen sat behind me and started pulling every braid out of my hair. He rolled his window down and threw every braid out of the window. I know you may be in disbelief reading this, but this is the life of an Autism Mom.

You may be asking, "Why didn't you put on the child proof locks?" Jaycen would have broken the window if he felt that you were restraining him. If I had stopped, he would have run out along the interstate. God told me to keep driving, so with tears in my eyes and a very sore scalp, I kept driving and never looked back. It was truly hard and humiliating but I stayed calm. Many times, I asked him to stop but when Jaycen feels he is getting to you, and he detects that he is making you angry, it makes him get more and more aggressive. My girls asked him politely, pleading with him to stop, but he didn't stop until every braid had been pulled out and thrown out of the window.

There were so many instances where our lives could have ended tragically. Jaycen on several occasions have grabbed the steering wheel from me and pulled the car out of gear. It is sad because some children with autism have no fear. Danger is not in their vocabulary. I am so thankful to God for me and my family's safety over the years, because he has placed his hands of protection over us.

I will never forget when I was trying to enroll Jaycen at a treatment program in Birmingham. I was denied because the facility didn't have a professional whose expertise was in autism. Jaycen became very irate as we waited and attempted to attack me at the treatment center right in front of a police officer. When Jaycen got disturbed and his anger was elevated he became very strong. The police officer had to restrain him by cuffing his hands and feet to a chair.

I hated to see my son in this situation, but he needed help. Jaycen was so strong, jumping up high, he lifted himself and the chair up in the air attempting to fight the police officer. I was so thankful that they remained calm because they were very aware of his mental illness. One of the police officers asked, "How in the hell can this mother take care of her son in this condition?" "She has to get him some help!" I would often cry out to God to give me and my girls some relief. It was truly hard for us, but I was very grateful for my family's support in helping me with my children.

Being a single mom with three children was very challenging and it took so much out of me having to deal with Jaycen. We truly had a rough time with him but when he was in a good mood, he was very loving and caring towards us. He loved his Ma to death! My autism prince watched my every move and when he saw a man around me, he would literally become overprotective of me and the girls. His behavior was excellent when he was consistently taking his medication. I loved his behavior. Although it took twenty years, I was so thankful that we had finally found the right treatment program for Jaycen in Montgomery, it was all in God's perfect timing.

Jaycen was a non-verbal child, but he had a huge impact on me and my Mom's estranged relationship. He had a special bond with his Grandma. My Mom and everyone else spoiled him rotten. Jaycen was the common link that helped softened and eased the tension of our relationship. When we were left in the same room together, Jaycen and the rest of the grandchildren were what we talked about the most. God has a way of bringing relationships closer together. There is a purpose for everyone.

Chapter Fourteen

BLESSINGS IN THE MIDST OF A STORM

I got a call from the school administration offering me a position as a special need paraprofessional at the middle school. God works in mysterious ways. I was so thankful that through all my storms, God blessed me with a rainbow. I didn't have any experience in teaching, but I knew that this opportunity would educate me on mental illness and autism. God blessed me with exactly what I asked for and more! I asked him for knowledge about my son's illness and a team to support me.

God saw fit to improve my finances by blessing me with a job too! Later I found out that Dr. Tera Simmons, a school administrator saw me working with my son at a department store and felt that my experience with my own son would be a perfect fit as a special needs teacher. I was so happy that God had me in the right place at the right time.

I will be forever grateful for Dr. Simmons and her act of kindness. She truly blessed me. When we are facing storms in our lives, you never know how God will make our crooked places straight and work on situations to put us in a better place. Dr. Simmons and her entire family has been a blessing in my life. They are the sweetest and most lovable people you would ever want to meet.

Her Mom, Mrs. Dale Simmons was a beautiful woman of God. She extended an invitation to me years ago to visit their church where her husband is the pastor. I truly enjoyed Sunday service at their church, and I often prayed to God to continue to bless their family. Sadly, Mrs. Dale passed away in the spring of 2021. She will truly be missed, and her legacy will forever live in our hearts.

Working in special education has been a blessing, and it is really like I am surrounded around my family. I understand my son and his illness a lot better. Being a special education teacher has helped me to gain knowledge and an understanding of my son's autism and many other delays. I never applied for the teaching position at the school. After being offered employment, I went to the school and filled out an application. I started my new position as a para-professional teacher in special education the next week.

Thank you, Jesus! I loved my new job! I worked with students that had dyslexia, lacked social skills, and mental illness issues, but none like my son Jaycen. I enjoy working with my students. It was a breath of fresh air for me being at work escaping the violence. I would often go to work with bloody bruises from fighting with Jaycen and exhaustion from lack of sleep. I worked with wonderful teachers that knew my situation and they always kept me encouraged, they truly became my family. Going to work every day felt like I was working in my purpose.

Working in the school district has allowed me to gain wonderful relationship with my students, staff, and parents. They say when you are passionate about what you do, it doesn't seem like work. Working with the students in special education is not an easy task, but it is very rewarding. When a parent sees the progress in their child's ability to tie their shoes, get potty-trained, learn to write their names for the first time, count or say their ABC's, it brings them so much joy.

I take my responsibility as a teacher very serious because I know the positive impact that my own children's teachers left on them. I treat my students just like my own, if they walk and are about to fall, I am there to catch them. If they are having trouble feeding themselves, I make sure I am available to assist. They don't struggle for anything. I know I can be overbearing because I seem more anxious to protect my students sometimes more than their own parents. For some reason, I stay in protection mode of mine and other people's children. A lot of my actions with my children is because of what happened to me as a little girl. Even though my daughters never experienced having slumber parties and sleep overs, sometimes they stayed overnight with their Grandma, and I wasn't 100% comfortable with that.

At school I am always watching the little girls and boys and their interactions with each other. I monitor them closely when they have restroom breaks because I want to make sure everyone stays protected. When you are violated against your will it is very hard to trust anyone. You always feel someone is out to get you. I am more like a Mother to my students. They can come and talk to me about anything.

Children should stay children as long as they can. I felt robbed of my childhood. I never experienced the true essence of being a child, it was cut short. Like making new friends, school field trips, participating in school activities, learning new hobbies, going to basketball and football games, school dances, and the prom. I never got a chance to experience any of that. Not having a positive upbringing can affect a child's overall sense of being. Early childhood trauma will affect a child's development and may also influence what kind of people they gravitate towards.

Surrounding yourself around the right people is very important. As a child your parents try to keep you away from the troublemakers because sooner or later their harsh behaviors may start rubbing off on you. Your parents love you and want the best for you. Having a circle of good friends helps build positive and long-lasting relationships. The saying, "You are what you eat," and "Watch the company that you keep," are all metaphorical expressions, but there are certain truths to these statements.

For instance, if you don't eat healthy foods, you won't be healthy. In order to become healthy and fit you must exercise and have a healthy balanced diet. If not, you may feel mentally, emotionally and physically exhausted, which could eventually create health issues. Eating healthy can be challenging but doable. I am working on having better eating habits.

It is very critical to watch who you chose to be around in your friendships. Sadly, you are judged by the people that you associate yourself with. If you hang around people that make bad choices, because of peer pressure you may start mimicking some of their ways. There is so much in life to help create a better you. What are you doing to pursue your God-given potential? Most of us won't ever know our gifts and talents unless we try something new. Be unafraid and explore every opportunity.

Some of the nerds and overachievers that you laughed at in school are now your bosses. We are all given the same number of hours in a day. Your time is precious, and it is important not to waste it on frivolous things. While you may be hanging out doing nothing productive, someone else is following their dreams of becoming a successful entrepreneur, furthering their education, networking with investors, joining the military, and building wealth for themselves and their families.

Visualize your best self, then start showing up as him or her. Life is too precious to waste it on people that don't add value to your life. A lot of your buddies spend their day doing absolutely nothing. Some people have no ambitions and goals and don't want to see you with any. Be yourself. Make a plan. Write it down. Take action.

Chapter Fifteen

911, WHAT IS YOUR EMERGENCY?

I am so thankful for God's protection. I sit and think about how my girls, and I stayed in the house most of the time fearful that if we went out Jaycen would hurt himself or others. We would drive through downtown Greenville, and when I pulled up to a traffic light, Jaycen would unlock the door, get out of the car and start running in traffic. It was the scariest moments of my life, because I was so afraid, he would get hit. I pulled the car over with my girls inside and chased my son in the street. Jaycen should have run on the track team because he could run so fast.

My heart would be beating very fast as I was running, screaming and crying. I was constantly yelling, "Jaycen please stop! Please stop!" No one bothered to help me catch him, but thankfully he got too tired to keep running and eventually I caught up with him. We walked back to the car, and I chastised him, but because he was non-verbal, he only grunted back at me, but he knew he was in trouble. There were times when I couldn't catch him, and I would immediately dial 911. I was thankful that they knew my situation of having an autistic child and knew how to handle him.

I had two girls but most of my time was spent with Jaycen. I constantly apologized to my girls for not always being able to spend quality time with them. I missed out on doing fun mother and daughter outings together. I felt the mom guilt, it was like they were being punished for their brother's autism. Thankfully, my girls were very supportive of their brother. They empathized with me, and I was happy that they never blamed me or their brother for having to live this way.

Sometimes I would keep my girls out of school just to help me take care of Jaycen. He was more than a handful and everyday his behavior got worse and more aggressive. My daughters would always try to help, but I was scared that he would hurt them. When Jaycen knew that he was making us mad, he felt like he was winning the battle. We always had to keep our cool, even when we were in pain, because if we didn't react, eventually he would stop.

I kept the police department's number on speed dial. One day Jaycen had left home for hours. Later I got a call from a police officer telling me that Jaycen was found many miles away from home. A minister from Florida was driving through the town when Jaycen just walked out in front of his car. Thankfully the minister was able to stop on brakes in time without hitting him. We would often have to barricade ourselves in the house, by pushing the washer and dryer to the back door and moving the sofa and love seat against the front door to keep Jaycen from running away.

For years I slept on the sofa by the front door, fearful that he would run away if I slept in my bed. He knew how to unlock our doors, but when I attempted to change to different locks that wasn't easy to unlock, I was told by the fire department that it was against the fire code.

Life with Jaycen was very unpredictable. Most days I was worried, stressed, uptight, fearful and full of anxiety. I always had to be ready to tackle his aggressive behaviors. We tried our best to keep a normal routine which would include, low lighting in the house, quiet sounds, some of his favorite foods, positive attitudes, and an overall regular daily routine. We stayed in the house as much as possible because Jaycen hated being in large crowds. When Jaycen was in a good mood, he was very affectionate. He loved to cuddle in my arms like a baby. It was like he was 16 years old with a 5-year-old mind.

In some non-verbal children with autism that may have aggressive behaviors, it is not uncommon that they may have underlining illnesses that they can't verbalize. For example, gastrointestinal pain, such as vomiting, acid reflux, abdominal pain, constipation, and diarrhea. These issues can affect a child's sleep and inability to learn.

Jaycen often was frustrated, and his irritability caused him to not have a good sleep pattern and frequent behavior issues. These symptoms may also cause them to harm themselves or others if the pain is unbearable. It is important to always monitor your child's behavior closely and if you suspect they are in pain, schedule a doctor's appointment immediately. Hopefully then the pain is gone, and they are able to get their behaviors back on track so that they can relax, learn, engage, and behave appropriately

Chapter Sixteen

My Daughters Are My Angels on Earth

My daughters Jordyn and Jazmine are my pride and joy. When I got pregnant with my girls, I got criticism from a family member that I won't ever forget. It is sad when family has a negative opinion about how you rear your children but will help a total stranger before putting forth effort to help you. I was a teenage mother and I never asked or was looking for a handout from anyone. A lot of the older adults seem to forget the mistakes they made as a young adult. They didn't always do things the right way but will be quick to criticize someone else.

People should understand that no matter what present status you're at, it doesn't make you better than others. Yes. I know I could have made some different choices, but I did what I did. Maybe if I had a better foundation laid out for me as a child, my life would have turned out differently. What Christ gives us is hope that the future will be better than the past or present. He knows that the hurts you go through in life may slowly rob you of who you think you are, and who you want to be. I have moved on with my life and I am thankful to God that he has truly matured me with no regrets.

My girls are truly a blessing in my life. They helped me tremendously with their brother Jaycen. I had a lot of Mama's guilt because Jordyn, my oldest daughter truly missed out on her childhood and teen years of having fun with her friends. There were no proms, dances, movies, and gatherings with her friends because she was always home helping me with Jaycen.

I leaned on Jordyn for everything, sometimes even having her miss school to help out because it was truly a struggle with Jaycen and I couldn't do it alone. Jordyn was a kid, but she had so many adult responsibilities when it came to her brother. She never complained but did it willingly. She would often express to me how she was concerned about me and my depression and mental health.

Jaycen viewed her as a second Mom, he had no idea that he was the oldest and the girls were his little sisters. When Jaycen wanted something, he would pull Jordyn's hand and guide her to what he wanted, then he would point to it. She absolutely loved her little big brother. I want the best for my daughters because they have been through a lot, and I can see so much potential in both of them. Jordyn always had a desire to pursue a career in the military. She talked about it often as a child. In middle school she was very quick on her feet because she loved to run track. We would drive all over the state of Alabama for track meets.

Jordyn is a beautiful girl and I've always admired her strength and athleticism. When I look at my daughter, I see so much of me. I have an open relationship with both of my daughters because I want them to know that they can talk to me about anything. Jordyn is like a second mother to her brother and my baby girl Jazmine. She learned exactly what to do at an early age for her brother, giving him his medicines daily. Jaycen takes about 25 to 30 pills a day and she knew all of them by heart.

I think about how my life would have turned out if I had that same open-door policy with my Mom, like I have with my girls. I wouldn't have had so many trust issues, paranoia, low self-esteem, and lack of confidence and difficulties with finding and receiving true love. It is very important for me to tell my daughters how they make me proud, tell them that they are beautiful and compliment them frequently, so they won't have to get validation from a boy.

As the elders would say, it was hard for me not to give in to every Tom, Dick, and Harry because they gave me the attention that I desired from my family. I am so happy that God has blessed me with wisdom to instill in my daughters how important it is to respect your body. I know they are not perfect and will make mistakes, but no matter what, I will always be there for them.

My oldest daughter Jordyn loved running track. One day I drove her to a track meet, and she had a seizure in the car! I was scared to death, and I didn't know what to do because I hadn't ever seen this before, especially with my daughter. I kept driving with one hand on the steering wheel and the other holding her chest until I made it to the hospital. Thankfully it was a mild one. She ended up being fine but was diagnosed with having a Grand Mal seizure.

I was so thankful after we made it to the hospital that it was confirmed that there was no negative activity affecting her brain. After the seizure she fell asleep. Weeks later our way to another track meet she had another seizure and that was the end of her running track in middle school. It was a hard decision for her, but she knew her health was being compromised.

Although Jordyn went through a lot with her brother, she still worked hard to graduate from high school. Jordyn has a lot of potential. I am so proud how hard she works and was able to purchase her very first car on her own. She is very smart, and I am really excited to see her pursue her dreams, and experience life for herself as a thriving young adult.

We have open communication with each other but sometimes my opinions cause her to be frustrated with me. No matter what, I pray that she realizes that her greatness is right around the corner and if she continues to work hard, she will be blessed with whatever her heart desires. There is so much that Jordyn has to offer the world and I want to see her pursue her God fulfilled purpose.

Jazmine, my youngest daughter is my little artist. She loves to draw and paint. As a child, she was truly a busy body. In the 2nd grade her art teacher noticed her artistic potential immediately. Without even knowing it, Jazmine had entered her drawings on an online art website while only 7 years old. She also loves community service and for Christmas, that same year, she made hundreds of personalized greeting cards with her artworks and mailed them to the troops. Jazmine's art goes beyond just drawings, she absolutely loves animations.

My baby girl is an entrepreneur. At only 19 years old she has her own business offering customized themed art and clothing. She is working towards becoming a professional illustrator. Jazmine didn't have a full schedule with her brother like her sister Jordyn. Her schedule was a lot more flexible, which enabled her to do fun things in high school. She was able to hang out with her friends and participate in many school extracurricular activities. I was often fearful that Jordyn would be envious of her sister's freedom. Thankfully she never showed any of those signs, just helped where it was needed.

Jazmine is very outgoing and a lover of life. She had goals and a go-getter spirit at a very young age. I love how she expresses her creativity through her paintings. When she paints, she does it effortlessly as she brings the colors altogether to make a beautiful canvas. I know with her talents and passion for the arts she will go far.

I love the bond that my girls share with their Grandma. They love her dearly, and it is truly a blessing to see how my Mom interacts with them. It makes me proud to see how God is transforming my Mom. She is much more lovable and attentive to her family's needs. I love the growth that I see in her. My girls mean the world to me. I pray that they will be able to succeed and not allow distractions to hinder their success.

I want them to know that they are beautiful, loved unconditionally, and worthy of having the best life. I am beyond proud to be called their Mama. I am happy to see their independence, always keeping God first, thinking positive and staying focused. I will always encourage them to love themselves first, and remember to stand up, speak up and never give up.

Chapter Seventeen

Don't Let Others Define Who You Are

Being a Mother is my first priority and has always been to love and protect my children. I am now an empty nester and God has given me the green light, that the time is right. My God is so awesome! Speaking on your truth can definitely be therapy. It gives you strength and power and you start believing in yourself. It helps you to gain your self-worth and confidence back. You discover that you have a purpose in life.

No matter how I tell my truth, even if it is done in love, there will be some that will hate me, but I must be honest and learn to take better care of me and my mental state. This journey of mine hurts and I haven't completely healed.... but God! Although man may disappoint you, God never will. In doing your best, sometimes you must be a disappointment to people. Many people are eager to please others, they want to be portrayed in this image and in the course of it all, they disobey God. The ways of God is not always popular to people.

In some of the Holy Scriptures, many people that God used had been rejected by their peers. It is ok to be different. Noah was a laughing stock when he built Noah's Ark. Moses was despised by his own and cast off by his adopted family. Jacob was rejected for his tricks, and Joseph was sold to slavery by his brothers.

As the saying goes, "When man disappoints you, God appoints you." When I look over my life, I can truly say I've been blessed to have had some genuine, anointed, and God-fearing people to tell me that my life has purpose. My story is important. My dreams count. My voice matters. I was born to make an impact. I have always felt that God had a bigger purpose for my life. I love teaching, but I know my greater is coming. Sometimes you just need a little push to get you going, but in my case, I needed several big pushes.

In your life, loving someone may mean letting them go. If you are friends with someone but having them as a friend is a constant battle, you may have to cut all ties. People can only take from us what we allow. Having a positive mindset and respect for others is the key to building successful relationships. Be complete within yourself. Never compete with others. We dwell on what we see on the outside, but we don't always know the whole story. What obstacles did that person have to go through to get to where they are today? We are so focused on how they are shining but their light may have been dim for years.

When we compare ourselves to others, we feel that we are less than, which may take away the joy in our own lives. Competing and comparing ourselves to others also leads to jealousy, stress, and exhaustion. Sadly, women compete with other women everyday constantly counting others blessings when they should be focusing on their own. Life will not hand us everything. If wealth wasn't passed down to us, we must work hard for what we want.

Learn to empower, inspire, and uplift one another. Life is not a competition; it is our own unique journey. Let's make ourselves a point of reference and compete against our previous self to be better than we were before. Focus on what really matters and silence the external noise. Compete not with others, for who we choose to be our competition may just be our footstool.

I have always danced to the beat of my own drums; I enjoy running my own race. If we admire someone, don't look at them as our enemy, we can gain knowledge and wisdom from them. We can learn from each other, because we are better together. Know that there are more than enough blessings for everyone, so someone else's gain is not your loss.

Do you know that God wants us to have an abundant life? Living in abundance means seeking after God and his goodness. He wants you to make the most out of every opportunity and live a good life. Build up your imagination, it is your faith. Stop asking God for itty bitty blessings when we have a bigger than life God. Let's pray, work hard and believe in God for what we want, and remember the blessings will come in his timing.

We are children of God and our father possess all the riches, so why can't we? God says, "Ye have not because you ask not." It doesn't matter what our family backgrounds look like, we may be the one to change the narrative for our families. We must be careful with sharing our plans with others. Steve Harvey stated, "If you want to kill a big dream tell a small- minded person."

Stop letting people talk you out of your goals. Imagination is a preview of what God has for you. Nothing is too hard for God. The United Negro College Fund's slogan is "A mind is a terrible thing to waste, but a wonderful thing to invest in." Education is believed to be the most important tool to make you successful in today's society. However, a man without a dream or vision shall perish according to the Bible.

Most of my life I have been staying quiet, keeping to myself and making everyone around me happy, but what about Jacquie? This is my season for grace and favor. I want to free my mind because sometimes I feel like I am stuck with a hole in my heart. I just want to be happy again.

Happiness is an emotional state characterized by feelings of joy, satisfaction, contentment, and fulfillment. Happiness is a choice. It is controlling your emotions with more positive thoughts than negative. It is remembering that we cannot be happy always pleasing others. We don't have to get validation from others. It could get stressful trying to be better than someone else or always worrying about what we did or didn't do, because that is not the will of God.

God has given us our own path; he knows us better than we know ourselves. How others may perceive us isn't necessarily factual but only an opinion. Their opinion doesn't matter in the eyes of God. Some people may think you are too mean, too loud, and lack love for others. They are always being judgmental towards you but remember you will always be perfect for you.

People can be very critical when they don't know your story. Sometimes it is a lack within themselves that they try to criticize you with hurt, anger and malice. Maybe they aren't happy with their own life and will attempt to bring negativity to yours. It is so important to be happy for others, because your blessings may be right around the corner. You may be doing something that they never had the courage to do. Their attempt to hurt you will make them feel good about themselves.

God doesn't want us to be jealous of others, as I have stated before, it is enough blessings for all of us. We should live with the mindset that we are blessed to be a blessing. It is nothing like helping others during their time of need. So many people have been a blessing to me, and my family and I have helped so many and never gotten anything in return, but God knows our heart. Learn to help others behind closed doors, your good deed doesn't have to always be broadcasted.

Some people only help others just to get credit. Helping others is what we are supposed to do. Our reward and praise will come from God. When we show generosity to others and not expect anything in return, it brings joy to us and God. Always encourage yourself even when no one else does.

I remember growing up, I felt that if I could only, please my Mom, and live up to the standards of others, I would be loved more. No matter how many mistakes you have made, God continues to love us. Repent of your sins, love yourself, speak victory over your life and stay in faith. They say that God gives his toughest assignments to his strongest soldiers. Be ready for the battle.

Chapter Eighteen

TAKE CONTROL OF YOUR MENTAL HEALTH

I was asked by a friend what would be the biggest take-away that I have learned from my journey. There are so many things like, taking care of your psychological, emotional, physical and social well-being. Forgiving others and yourself and learning how to communicate effectively. Another important thing that a lot of people ignore is taking care of their health. Our health should always be our top priority. Eating balanced and healthy meals will eliminate fatigue and help you to live a long-lasting life.

Learning how to take a break when we need to, and saying "No," when feeling overwhelmed can be helpful in boosting our mental health. No one knows us better than we know ourselves. We must do what's needed to have a positive mental state. I had thoughts of giving up my parental rights because it was so stressful dealing with my son. It was so hard for me that I didn't care about getting compensated monthly from the state. It was never about the money, I love my son dearly, but I needed a stress-free life. My mind could never relax and be at peace.

It was hard for me to go to sleep because Jaycen stayed up throughout the night. He would be roaming around the house which kept us all uneasy. I was constantly told by a state agency that in order to place him in a state facility that I would have to give up all my rights.

Thinking back, all I truly wanted was to get my son the help that he needed and well deserved. I still wanted to be his Mom because he was mine. I dreaded to have conversations with the agency because they showed no empathy for me. I knew that I couldn't properly take care of Jaycen because I couldn't handle his aggressive behavior and I was fearful that he would hurt me and my girls.

Having a child with autism is exhausting and going through the back and forth with the state agency, I was ready to let him go. My son needed professional help that I couldn't give him. After speaking with my boss Principal Joseph Dean, Special Education Teacher Richard Kelly, and the Special Education Coordinator Willie Thornton, they really helped me sort things out and realize that I couldn't let my son go.

My mental health was truly being compromised. My journey was filled with suicidal thoughts. I didn't want to live anymore. I was ready to give up. I needed to heal from my past and was so stressed in the present. So many times, I just wondered would anyone miss me if I was gone, but honestly, my kids brought me through every time. They gave me a reason to want to live and not die. I was a drained parent. I was tired! God knew I needed an advocate; these men gave me the assurance to help me make my decision. I owe them a plethora of gratitude for being a listening ear. I am so grateful for the love and concern they had for me and my family. They truly helped me put everything into perspective.

I will never forget that day, I was so ready to give up, but they all knew that's not what I really wanted. They knew I needed help because my son is literally everything to me. I eat, sleep, and breathe that boy of mine. I really felt like he was gifted to me by God, which was all part of his beautiful plan.

Jaycen and his diagnosis of autism has truly changed my life and I hope to change someone else's life for the better. I want to learn more and do more to help educate the community. I want others to find peace in knowing that greater days are coming. After my conversations with the guys, a voice whispered to me saying, "Keep fighting," "Keep pushing," "Never give up!" Therefore, I will always be an advocate for Autism Awareness. I remember how happy I was when I got the call from the treatment program. I am happy to report that Jaycen is calm and loving now, he is totally a different person. I am very thankful that God answered my prayers.

So many needs support and like me at the beginning, you are clueless about what to expect with your autistic child. The beauty of my story is that God gave me the will power to be the voice for my child who is voiceless. I have confidence and love for myself, and I am getting closer to open my heart to forgive. I have never wished for any other life, because I know we all have some form of challenges. It is funny how some may think that the grass is greener on the other side, but the grass is greener wherever you water it. I'm still learning this.

There are many people in the world existing, but not living. Do what you love, and success will follow you. Passion is the fuel behind a successful career. Taking care of ourselves and our mental health is essential to having a happy and healthy lifestyle. We are living our lives worried, stressed and depressed. Young adults are having heart attacks at alarming rates because we aren't getting regular check-ups at the doctor's office. Stop making excuses and go to the doctor. Our health is our wealth. I know I have mentioned this before, but it is so important that we take better care of ourselves. Learn to invest in your health and your family's health.

We must learn to better our overall well-being. When you start a new job whether it is self-employment or working for a company make sure you take advantage of getting life insurance. Some life insurances have a cash value that allows you to save for retirement while having coverage. Young people may think this is a benefit for the older generation, but no one knows the day nor the hour. It is sad when your loved one dies and a financial burden is placed on the family to give the deceased a proper burial.

This lack of preparation can pose a negative effect on your mental health. You must resort to raising money which can cause you to feel embarrassed and regretful. It helps if you purchase coverage early because life insurance gets more expensive as you get older and your health changes. Consult with a financial planner and start paying for the peace of mind that comes from financially protecting your family.

Having open communication about our feelings can help us stay in a positive mental state to deal with times that we may feel troubled. Remember if we're not speaking it, we're storing it. This is when an individual may allow situations to get out of control and will cause them to do the unthinkable. Staying active, eating well, taking breaks, getting plenty of sleep, showing kindness and respect for ourselves and others, traveling, coloring, writing and keeping a journal helps you to have a healthy lifestyle.

Managing stress levels, reading, surrounding ourselves around positive people are also ways to improve our health and wellness. Give yourself permission to take a mental health wellness day to relax and recharge. Everybody is not our assignment, that's why we are so drained. We're not "Bob the Builder," we can't fix everybody's problems.

Be there for your loved ones but don't let others walk all over you. Stop glorifying being busy all the time and get some rest. Trying to prove to your boss and peers that you can do every job better than others, will only lead to you being burnt out, overwhelmed, and possible health issues. If you get sick and unable to perform your duties, understand that you are replaceable. We always want to do our very best at school, work, church, or in the community, but we must take care of ourselves first, because if we don't no one else will.

Let's monitor what we are indulging into our spirit. Listen to music that will speak positively to our souls, watch TV programs that will uplift and inspire us. Although celebrities shouldn't be our ultimate role model, sometimes lyrics in songs and TV programs and podcast can influence someone to mimic others' behaviors, whether it is good or bad. There is so much devastation going on in the world with police brutality, human sex trafficking, political bias, poverty and homelessness, violence, racism and injustices. Although it is necessary to be informed, it can be depressing and damper our mood if we watch too much of the same thing. Set limits to your news watching to keep your mental health in a wellness state.

Activities like running in the park, turning your phone on the "Do Not Disturb" mode, taking a hot bath, taking a break from social media, participating in school and church activities, signing up for a pottery or painting class may help you enjoy your life better.

Meditating is also helpful to reclaim your quality time back. Taking the time to not worry about deadlines, just calming down and focusing on your breathing is huge. As a teacher it can get very stressful and a quick break from your students is necessary. Limiting your sugar intake and finding healthier ways of snacking is a great way to take control of your mental health. Cutting back on foods high in sugar like sodas, candies, and cakes won't cure depression, but it will help your health and keep your blood sugar levels stable. This helps balance your energy levels throughout the day.

When I haven't eaten the right foods, my body immediately will let me know. I am too full, tired and sluggish, and only want to lay down and rest. Eating foods that are high in magnesium like almonds, whole wheat bread, peanut butter, dark chocolate, figs, black beans, yogurt, bananas, raisins, apples, carrots, avocados and brown rice are helpful in alleviating headaches and fatigue.

Another good indicator of taking care of our mental health and wellness is having good quality relationships. Are you the friend that is always giving and the other person is always taking? After spending quality time together do you feel happy and excited or drained and unfulfilled? Do your friends always find fault in everything that you do?

Don't entertain toxic partners, toxic friendships or toxic co-workers because they are truly bad for your health. Healthy relationships consist of compassion, sharing, caring, listening, love and kindness, freedom of thinking for yourself, healthy disagreements, security and safety. Toxic relationships are filled with insecurities, criticism, dishonesty, selfishness, abuse of power and control, high tempers and attitudes, jealousy and negativity.

Toxic behaviors can lead to verbal and physical abuse and could affect your mind, body, and soul. Change your thinking and don't be trapped, believe that you deserve to be treated with love, kindness and respect.

Sometimes we can't un-hear what a person have said or un-feel the hurt they've caused, especially when they never apologized. I'm a good person who loves unconditionally. I care about people in a way they will never be capable of understanding. The hurt I endured led me to choose me. I choose me this time. I am a very private person. I have pretended for years to be okay simply because I didn't want to annoy others with my problems.

I have prayed for the day that I can walk in my purpose and not feel ashamed. I am ready to take Jacquie to the next level. I am worthy of everything God has for me. I don't care about how others perceive me anymore. My life doesn't have to be defined by what others think about me. Our mind will always believe what we tell it. Feed it faith. Feed it truth. Feed it love. The trials of life have given me strength and hope for a better tomorrow.

God's endings are always better than his beginnings. It feels so good to finally learn how to take good care of ME! When I am overwhelmed and feeling discouraged, I enjoy reading my favorite book by Mary Monroe entitled "God Don't Like Ugly" and "God Still Don't Like Ugly!" I'm a huge fan of poetry, and I enjoy Poet, Civil Rights Activist, Author and Actress Maya Angelou. My favorite poem is "Phenomenal Woman."

I absolutely love listening to music. There's something about listening to good music that helps decrease the stresses of life. I love Lauren Hill, my favorite song is called "Zion." H.E.R. is another one of my favorite artists, her song "Damage," is very relatable to my story. I enjoy listening to Ed Sheeran, my favorite is his song "Photograph." Through self-growth, self-care, and self-love, my mindset has shifted, and I am ready to be all that I can be!

I Am Becoming the Best Version of Me

Where I'm going, I'm sorry but you can't go with me
Negativity, hurt, pain, stress, depression
You can't go with me
I'm finally able to smile
Tears you can't go with me
I'm finally able to love
Heartbreak you can't go with me
I'm finally able to breathe
Anxiety you can't go with me
I'm finally comfortable in the skin I'm in
Shame you can't go with me
I'm finally owning everything I've done
Regret you can't go with me
I am finally at peace with my life
And I'm taking this joy I've found with me

Chapter Nineteen

ALL WE NEED IS LOVE

One of the most common relationship issues people face today is the struggle to express love in meaningful ways to someone else. I am very grateful for the love my Mom and I are now sharing and everyday our relationship seems to get stronger and stronger. My Mom was brought up in a generation where there wasn't much open communication between families about certain topics.

I don't feel my Mom was truly taught how to love. I don't recall getting hugs and kisses as a child, having conversations about how my day is going or how she was doing. I don't recall this ever happening. Growing up, we were told to leave the room when adults were talking. As the saying goes "Children should be seen but not heard." If a child wanted to state an opinion about anything they were looked at as being sassy and was quickly put in their place.

I know my Mom loves me and she did the best at the time. Not discussing the situation with me about being raped and acting like it didn't happen was the best way she knew how to handle it. As an adult, I can see my Mom for who she really is. Sometimes the bad things that happen in our lives put us directly on the path to the best things that will ever happen to us.

My Mom is loving, smart, caring, funny, hard-working, very supportive of me, her children, grandchildren and my non-profit organization. She always tries to make people happy, and with everything she has been through, she continues to keep a smile on her face.

There is no judgment because I realize that some people demonstrate love and care for one another differently. Everything that I wanted my Mom to do for me as a little girl, I see her doing for my girls. It brings me so much joy and happiness. Nobody is perfect and I am thankful to be able to see her blossoming into her role as a Grandma. She absolutely loves her grandchildren, and they love her.

As my Mom has gotten older she is much wiser. I can see a change in her between her children and her grandchildren. I am thankful that our relationship is much better. We are more open with one another, and it feels so good. I pray that we can one day have an open conversation about the day my innocence was taken from me. At 40 years old, I feel like I am still trapped in an 11-year-old little girl's body.

The year 2022 will be exactly 30 years of me living with this secret. It is sad but too many sexual predators get away with rape and molestation and take it to their graves while the victims mourn through life in silence. We can no longer be silenced! Telling your story will heal the world. I thank God for my Mom and Grandma's prayers, and anyone else that had it in their spirit to pray for me.

So many people are healing from things that they haven't discussed with anyone. Sometimes people can't heal because they keep pretending, they're not hurt. With tears in my eyes, I sit and think of the lyrics of Dorothy Norwood's gospel song, "Somebody Prayed for Me." "Somebody prayed for me, had me on their mind, took the time and prayed for me. I'm so glad they prayed, I'm so glad they prayed, I'm so glad they prayed for me."

It is hard to explain the scars I have had to carry all these years. I could have gone mad, insane, crazy, or deranged…. but God! It is easy for others to say, "Get over it." I pray none of my family and friends have to endure this type of pain. I am thankful that the God I serve loves me and is working in me and through me. He delights in me, and I will always speak of his goodness. I often wonder what my life would have been like had I not endured the sexual abuse from my uncle. I probably wouldn't have had so many challenges to overcome. I know that God doesn't give us no more than we can handle, and my brokenness will be my breakthrough.

Let's protect our children! In your neighborhood, you may be living near a child predator. Every day they are preying on our helpless and innocent children. It is helpful to do your research online by typing in your zip code to see if a registered molester is in your area, and be careful because they may just be right in your family.

There are many useful steps to educate yourself about both sexual abuse and healthy sexual development in children. Like death, I know this is not something you want to think about, but it is happening to many children every day. I hate I am having to write about this, but I have done extensive research and if it will save a child from the pain I have experienced, I will keep writing, educating and speaking up for the innocent.

There are many signs that may suggest a child may have been a victim of sexual abuse. In younger children some signs may be imitation with sexual acts with toys, refusal to take off clothing at appropriate times, like bathing, or wetting the bed and sucking their thumb.

In older children and youth, anxiety or depression, self-harming behaviors or suicidal thoughts. Changes in self-care or paying less attention to hygiene, unhealthy eating habits, unusual weight gain, weight loss, or suddenly having money. Both may experience trouble sleeping, explicit sexual knowledge beyond the child's development stage, sudden or extreme mood swings (rage, anger, fear, crying, and withdrawals) pain, itching, or bleeding in genital areas.

Monitoring your children and creating a healthy environment is ways we show love and care to them. Always pay attention to what they are watching on TV and the friends they may be entertaining at school, home and on social media. In older children, have access to their phone code to make sure who they may be communicating with daily. It is also important to monitor computer games they may play that involves interaction with the outside world. Some children may have predators on the games and may also experience cyber-bullying. Cyber-bullying is real and contributes to a high percentage of teen suicidal rates.

When teens and youth experience bullying or cyber-bullying they engage in self-harm, have low self-esteem, and commit suicides. They may not tell you about it because they are fearful that you will make them stop playing the game, make the situation worse, or just too embarrassed to tell anyone. Stay involved with your children. Make sure you are not using their devices as a babysitter. This will make your child become addicted and create a bond with a total stranger. Be the parent and protect your children!

Sexual abuse can be touching and non-touching behaviors. Touching is an interaction between a child and an adult (or another child) in which the child is used for the sexual stimulation of the perpetrator or an observer. Non-touching behaviors may be trying to look at a child's naked body and/or exposing the child to pornography.

Child sexual abuse affects both girls and boys in all kinds of neighborhoods and communities. A child predator spends more time with children than adults. They are usually friendly and very affectionate. They come across as fun, easy-going, but immature and childish. They love to have a child sit on their lap. They love to mess with children that are loners and who looks troubled. Many child abusers are right in your own family or someone you know.

We live in a cruel world, don't allow your children to spend the night with any and everyone. Your children are your responsibility. Have a talk, build a relationship of trust and ask questions. I am on the road to healing because I don't break down as much and writing and talking about it is becoming much easier for me. I wanted to feel loved, but I never felt it and because of that I looked for love in all the wrong places. When situations like abuse aren't handled properly it can lead to a person feeling unwanted, helpless, and unloved.

Family love is a special type of love that comes with unique feelings, challenges, behaviors, and rewards. Healthy family love is unconditional. It is respect for one another through actions and words. It is providing effective communication, and as the parent, making sure everyone's physical and emotional needs are met until the children assume responsibility and becomes an adult and beyond.

Parents should always be careful when leaving their child alone with another adult or older child. If you have any suspicions about your child being sexual abused, first, please believe them, educate yourself and make sure they know you will be there to love and support them every step of the way.

As a single parent it can be very difficult at times, but it has gotten easier as my children has gotten older. I didn't get the love and support I had hoped for as a child, but I decided that I would constantly pour the love and acceptance into my own children, so they wouldn't have to deal with low self-esteem and lack of self-worth as I did.

It is sad to grow up thinking you are ugly and not have someone to esteem you and help develop you emotionally. We don't realize how important it is to tell our children that they are beautiful, worthy, you are proud of them through gestures, facial expressions and touch. This helps build their self-confidence, develop healthy bonds and will help strengthen their character. They will know that they can accomplish anything in life and be comfortable in knowing that they have their family's love and support.

If you lack giving your children praise and attention eventually it will make them suffer. Providing love and a stronger family support system helps increase family love, understanding, and communication skills. Some people think because you provide by going to work every day, buying food, providing shelter, and buying clothing for your children that's all you need to do to show them love. I know it helps but words are powerful and giving them the love and compassion that they need will help nurture your child's sense of self.

Giving your children compliments helps them gain confidence in knowing how to speak positively about themselves and showing self-love. Praise can boost them to work harder, help them stay positive in negative situations, and increase their motivation. Children need encouragement because just like adults they deal with challenges every day. As the parent, it is your responsibility to protect your children.

Just because your child is quiet it doesn't mean that everything is ok. They may be getting bullied at school and may blame themselves. They may be having trouble verbalizing what they are going through. Maybe they are struggling in their coursework or having trouble making friends. This is when you need to probe and ask questions making them comfortable enough to know that they can talk to you about anything.

When you become a parent, you must slow down and make sure your top priority is meeting your children's needs. Your dating life may have to be put on halt temporarily. It doesn't mean you don't deserve happiness and the potential to find love, but you want to make sure you stay involved with your children. No one ask to be a single parent, but you must embrace what life gives you and make the most of it. When the time comes for you to find your companion make sure he or she treats your children as a bonus instead of a burden.

As a parent you should be realistic with your child. Sometimes they may require some positive criticism with love, because you should be preparing them for the real world. If they lost a baseball game, did poorly on a test, or didn't make the top ten in the beauty pageant you should encourage them to keep trying and teach them that in life you will win some and lose some.

Teach them that they won't necessarily be good in everything because everyone has strengths and weaknesses. As parents we want to save our children from hurts and upsets, but this is how they learn and grow. Our children won't always make the best choices for their life. Don't be so quick to be a co-signer for your grown children or any family member. Teach them to earn their own way through obstacles.

I absolutely love hugs and kisses. Affection is a great way to show your child that you are proud of them. Studies show that giving hugs helps to increase a child's brain development as well as their overall social, emotional, and physical development. My children knows that their Mama doesn't hesitate to grab them and steal a hug and a kiss.

Affection between a child and a parent has been proven to help the child be happier, less anxious, and be able to create healthy emotional bonds in other relationships outside the immediate family. Love and affection have been known to also improve a child's academic performance, better the child and parent's communication, and they will exhibit fewer psychological and behavioral problems.

Love helps your child's mental well-being, makes them physically healthier, and helps them become less fearful and more secure in who they are. I hope and pray that my journey helps every family become closer in love.

Chapter Twenty

BIG BATTLES & BIGGER BLESSINGS

I have been told by so many people that I possess a certain quality in me, but I never saw it. I've been told that I was chosen to fulfill a duty, but I never knew it. No matter what blessings I receive, I will always still be me, no matter my wins or losses. I will never change who I am and that's what I love about fulfilling my purpose. You get to have me and something extra. I can see it and feel it now, I'm walking in my new journey. Although I have been working in special education for over a decade now, I truly feel that God has so much more for me. I am thankfully becoming the woman that God wants me to be.

I understand that my purpose is to minister to others. It doesn't necessarily mean having a church and being in a pulpit but working in the community. I believe that each one should teach one. When we walk in our purpose and overcome life's roadblocks, it is important to help someone else.

Years ago, I was hanging out with friends, and we went out to a bar. I was drinking and having a good time but when I went to the bathroom, I heard a young lady crying. She was telling me her life story of having low self-esteem, and not feeling accepted by family and friends. We were hugging and crying together. Her story was like mine. She truly didn't love herself and was battling with suicidal thoughts.

I had forgotten where I was and before I knew it, I started telling her how her life was worth living, how beautiful she was, and the plans that God has for her. Helping others will be how I want to be remembered. I commend people that go out of their way to lend a helping hand. I believe that it is our sole purpose in life. There have been many times that I have paid for someone's groceries or utility bill, because I remember the days that I have struggled.

A lot of Americans suffer from lack of food, but because of some unfortunate circumstances, they may not qualify for governmental assistance. It is a known fact that some adults and children go to bed hungry every night. It is truly a blessing when you have food banks available in your town to help bridge the gap of starvation.

There are so many worthy causes in the community that you can be involved in. Do your research and be a part of a replicable organization where you can volunteer. Consider volunteering with the senior citizens of your community. Some of them may not have family close by and a kind gesture like, a quick trip to the grocery store, preparing a hot meal, cleaning their home, or accompany them to their doctor's appointment may be what is needed.

I love participating in programs at the high school such as, "Adopt a High School Senior." Everyone remembers how expensive your senior year can be, with prom, school memorabilia, school rings, senior pictures, yearbook ads, test prep classes fees, college applications, and college enrollment and deposit fees. Our special education department always welcome supporters to help with classroom supplies, sensory equipment, cots for naps, or donation towards our annual special event the "Special Olympics." Your contribution can help purchase tents and many other accessories needed to make the event a continued success.

Honestly, I don't know where my new journey is going to take me but I'm going. I pray for wealth in my health, happiness, and finances. I have always thought about why the rich get richer and the poor seems to get poorer. There are plenty of factors but after meditating on this, I concluded that it is the individual's attitude and mindset. Ask yourself is the glass half full or is the glass half empty?

I am responsible for every result in my life. If we want different results, then we have to change our thoughts and actions. We may have to change our circle of friends. It doesn't mean that we are better than them, but we may be going in a different direction. Expecting people to clap for you and bring you happiness doesn't always happen. You have to learn how to have your own self-confidence and find your happiness from within. Believe in yourself even when no one else does.

Fear is another thing that is holding us back from our destiny. It can overwhelm our lives like a thick cloud of darkness controlling our decision making and every move. So much of what we spend our life worrying about never even happens. You want to step outside of your comfort zone, but because you are so afraid of failure, you don't even try. Fear can be passed down from generation to generation. Times are different. You have more opportunities than your parents and grandparents did. Who will break the cycle?

Stop letting opportunities of greatness pass you by. Step out on faith and don't worry about what others may think. They don't have the courage to try something new and will talk you out of it. Remember having a mindset of worry, fear, and anxiety will put limits on your gifts and talents. Stop worrying about what could go wrong and start focusing on what could go right. I feel that everyone in life has the potential to be successful. Some sit and wait on opportunity and others go out and get it. Which one are you?

It is funny how people can be so quick to blame others when they didn't turn out the way they assume that they would. I know there are some that have been blessed to grow up in a loving family with assets and inheritance where they don't have to work as hard as others. For the ones like me that didn't have much growing up, we must work twice as hard to accomplish our goals in life.

Settling for being mediocre is not an option for me. I want to make a difference, be the change, successful, fulfill my purpose, and reach my highest potential. When a person knows better, they will do better and I often pray for wisdom and understanding every day. I love my community and I know God is preparing me to get out of my comfort zone. Sometimes you got to stand still and let God move.

The old Jacquie was fine with being behind the scenes. I have never wanted to be in the spotlight, but my plans aren't always God's plans. I want to travel and see the world, be a beckon of hope for the hopeless, a shining star for the lost, an advocate for the voiceless, and a mentor for a mentee.

We should always be happy to see others being blessed, because everyone deserves to be celebrated. It brings me much joy to see my co-worker get a promotion, a friend blessed to buy a new house, or a family member to get engaged. Everyone has their own path and as I have mentioned before, it is ridiculous to be competing with someone else. Run your own race. Your blessing may be right around the corner but because you are so caught up in someone else's life, your blessing may just pass you by.

Stop judging others on what your naked eye can see. You never know what people are dealing with behind closed doors. I have been beat and bruised by my son in the early mornings, arrive to work, and some of my peers never knew what I was going through. I didn't want to have my personal life interfere with my professional life, so it was business as usual for me.

Some of my co-workers may have assumed I had the best life ever. My goal was to keep it together, but it was getting very difficult. Some would even comment about how good I looked and that they never saw me wear the same thing twice. I always had a smile on my face, but deep down I was crying inside. Before arriving to school, I would clean myself up, apply some makeup to cover the bruises, comb my hair, put on my smell good, a cute outfit and drive to work like nothing ever happened.

My students would always show me love and it kept me going. We all have things that we are dealing with, but it is how you handle the situation. Instead of taking part in the daily gossip, take the time to have a daily prayer. The same person you are dogging out may be the same one that will have to come to your rescue.

How do we acquire generational wealth? The cycle of poverty must end today. It is not fun living from paycheck to paycheck. Change your thinking. Our children should live a better life than we did. Work hard, make wise choices and leave a legacy for your children. Everyone likes nice things, but it must be a balance somewhere. Create an environment of more than enough by watching your spending habits. Instead of always buying your children the latest sneakers, name brand clothing, and every toy on the market, consider investing in your children by saving money.

This is not just for you, but for me too. I'm seriously making some much needed changes in my life. I want to one day retire and not worry about how I will make it financially. It is so important to teach your children about personal finance, invest in their education, take advantage of life insurance, focus on a hobby, create a family business to pass down, invest in stocks and bonds, and focus on the later instead of always the right now.

It is easy to make excuses about not being taught about saving money, money management and investing in your future growing up, but there are many options available to make sure you and your family have financial security. We must work hard to build wealth in our communities for our children and children's children.

I started a social media women's empowerment group called Sparkle and Shine. This group consists of 33 women that are from different backgrounds, different cities and states and have never met, but they are all getting to know each other. They are women who have never been in my circle of friends but that was the beauty of it for me. I decided to bring us together because we all have similar stories. This awesome group of ladies were handpicked by me to inspire, encourage, and motivate them to be the best versions of themselves through Christ.

We discuss important topics such as our faith in God, relationships, self-esteem, finances, goals, marriages, living the single life, careers, education, hair, fashion, and beauty. I believe everyone in this group can benefit from one another. We play fun games such as, picking a person for a week, a stranger in the group and offer complimentary compliments each day. You never know what insecurities or low self-esteem someone is dealing with and it is a great way to keep each other uplifted.

I stepped out on faith and God has blessed me to become an entrepreneur and open my own event planning center. I have always wanted to start my own business and be my own boss. My event planning center will not only be for my events but will be opened to the community to use for special occasions at affordable prices. Despite all my struggles, God continues to bless me over and over again.

I was so happy to be featured on the front page of our local newspaper, The Greenville Advocate, in an article entitled, "Autism Speaks – Are You Listening?" The "I Love You to Pieces," Autism Awareness Charity Event raises awareness to improve understanding of this often-misunderstood medical condition. April kicked off Autism Awareness month and I was excited to bring this event to the community in honor of my son to educate many on the effects of autism. Due to an unforeseen accident, we had to cancel the event, but I am definitely looking forward to rescheduling it in the near future.

Months later I was happy that I was able to host a back-to-school event for my non-profit organization in honor of my son, called "Joining Jalen's Fight." There is so much I have done and want to continue to do in the community. Giving back to others is so fulfilling and it gives you a sense of purpose. It is a great way of showing your appreciation, not only in money, but in time. It allows you to get to know the citizens in the community better and you will feel good knowing that you are part of making a difference in the world.

Life is an adventure! Live it while you can. Remember you can never have today again, tomorrow only come once, and yesterday is gone forever. Work hard, play hard then live the adventure you create. Be grateful for the life God has given you. Always grab every opportunity to show your skills, talents, and experiences. Train your mind to dwell on things that will add purpose to your life. Stay committed and never give up!

Our challenges in life can be a steppingstone to manifest us into greatness. Let's reshape who we are and become our supreme self. Everyone may have experienced some form of sadness within their lives, either you will use it as an excuse or motivation. Live your life without guilt, learn to forgive yourself and others. Moving forward in our destiny requires us to live a guilt-free life. We are human beings and we do make mistakes.

It was July 4, 2021, for the first time, I confronted the sexual offender, child abuser, rapist, sexual violator, perpetrator, and child molester my uncle! After being asked to speak at a church, "I said yes," because I knew he would be there. I pondered over and over again about the topic to speak to the congregation about and God spoke to me on the subject of "Forgiveness!" I was so nervous, and even though I was fully prepared physically and mentally, I was an emotional wreck!

As I was getting dressed, I kept reciting what I was going to say in my head. I prayed all the way to church. When I arrived at church I sat towards the back, not making eye contact with anyone. When the emcee called my name, I jumped up like I was ready, but when I made it to the front, I saw him. I asked the Lord to be with me while I began speaking. I discussed how forgiveness isn't for the person who did you wrong, but for you. I referred to several scriptures in the Bible for clarification.

When I finished, I sat down but I wasn't relieved because I knew there was something else that had to be done. To me, the hardest thing is forgiving someone who I felt wasn't sorry. As the deacons started the offering, I saw my uncle get up and go out the side door. I placed my offering in the basket and I walked right out the door, because it was time, and I knew I wouldn't get another chance. I knew he went into the fellowship hall, so I opened the door and walked in. He was behind the counter sweeping the floor. He looked up, and I looked down. My hands were sweating, my heart was beating fast, and I felt a knot growing in my stomach, but I kept walking towards him.

I was scared up until the moment my eyes met his. I felt the protection like no other! God was truly standing with me. He had his loving arms wrapped around me. With my head held high and eye to eye contact I stated, "I forgive you!" I turned around quickly and proceeded to walk out as I heard him call my name. I kept walking because there was no need for a conversation, I said what needed to be said.

I got in my truck and drove away. I kept turning on the windshield wipers, but it wasn't raining, it was my tears! I was driving, crying, and still praying. Weeks afterwards I continued to cry tears of joy. Although I was crying, I felt so alive! 30 years of un-forgiveness in my heart. 30 years of lack of healing. 30 years of not feeling loved, the right way. 30 years of not having peace of mind. 30 years of not enjoying family time. 30 years of low self-esteem. 30 years of living in bondage. 30 years of feeling embarrassed and ashamed. 30 years of feeling like a hostage, always hiding from the perpetrator. 30 years of feeling like I am trapped in an 11-year-old little girl's body.

This courageous act of forgiveness was the hardest thing I have ever had to do in my life, but the most rewarding. Prayer and surrounding yourself around good people is a true blessing. Help us Lord. My heart is so heavy. If God did this for me, he will surely do it for you! Go ahead. Forgive! Forgive so that you will be forgiven! I forgive my Mom and my uncle! I am delivered! I have been set free! Free! Free to be me!

With God and the power of our minds we can shake away the hurt and guilty feelings that sometimes may encourage us to linger into a life of sin. Guilt kills the joys of our lives, and the constant battles in our minds can leave us stagnant. Learn to put the past behind you. The mind is a powerful God-given tool. It can make you or break you. Your mind can transform your hopes and dreams to inspire us, or it can enslave us to make bad decisions and have negative thoughts. Let's pray that we can join and utilize the power of the Spirit to guard our minds and help us to release to God all guilt and shame.

Dear Heavenly Father, I come to you with a humble heart seeking clarity and conviction. Lord, I pray that you will continue to guide me on a path of righteousness. I thank you for your hand of protection of the things seen and unseen. I want to tell the world that I understand that in our humanness we all make mistakes, and although the shame and hurt remains, I wholeheartedly forgive the ones that have done me wrong. I also forgive myself for wronging others. I pray that any wrongdoers repent of their sins and learn to forgive themselves. Thank you for your goodness and mercy towards us. I pray that thy will be done in our lives, and we can serve you with fullness and gladness, and rejoice in your glory. In Jesus name. Amen.

My story may not be your story, but if you have been sexually assaulted, a parent of a special needs child, suffer from low self-esteem, depression, and suicidal thoughts, fear and anxiety, struggle with forgiveness, hardships of being a single parent, don't feel loved and worthy, loss of loved ones, or any other issues that may pose a threat to you or your family, pray to God and ask for guidance, and speak up until someone you trust actively listens. "I Need Thee!"

ACKNOWLEDGEMENTS

I acknowledge God for giving me the vision and courage to write this book. I give him the glory, honor, and praise in all that I do and all that I have been through in my life.

Mothers are one of the first indications of the sovereignty of God. Thank you to my Mom for birthing me into existence. I pray that this book will be our guide to a journey of continued happiness, growth, understanding, forgiveness and love.

Thank you to my siblings for always being there for me when I needed you the most. My siblings are a little bit crazy, little bit loud, but a whole lot of LOVE. I love you JarKeith, Jarvis (JBo), and Janee.

Aunt Nancy Young, thank you for being an inspiration throughout my life. You were the light in my darkness. You were there when I was struggling and at my lowest and because of your loving heart, you always encouraged me to write and express my emotions. Thanks to you and the will of God I am still writing! I love you!

To my best friend in the whole wide world! E'licia Allen! It is so hard for me to put into words what you mean to me. You are more than a best friend; you are my sister! We have shared the good, bad, and ugly. I love how we are happy when we both succeed. Your support and love for me and my children is undeniably real. You stood in support and helped me to restrain my son on numerous occasions when his behavior was intense. You have been my shoulder to cry on, you listen to my problems, and always found ways to cheer me up. I love you!

Family can extend beyond one household, and I am very thankful and blessed to have my extended family. Thank you to all my aunts, uncles, cousins, church members, neighbors, co-workers and friends that have helped me and played a part in encouraging me to be the best that I can be. I appreciate your love and thoughtfulness.

To the City of Greenville, Greenville Fire and Police Departments, Butler County City School System faculty and staff, I am grateful for your immediate response and sincere support of me and my son throughout his childhood and adult years.

To that special someone that has always encouraged me to keep pushing every time I thought about giving up. I would like to say, "Thank you!" Your love and support will always remain in my heart.

Writing my first book has been both challenging, heartfelt and exhilarating, and I couldn't have done it alone. This book is my life story filled with my transparency of pain, passion and purpose. My deepest gratitude to the staff at SUSU Entertainment LLC. I am grateful for your dedication to this project, support and encouragement. You've inspired me to step out on faith and have turned our countless conversations into these pages which has served as a map to my journey, and I would not have reached this destination without you.

In Loving Memory

Daisy Cook Hamilton
November 25, 1917- December 6, 2000

You always told me to do what's right,
whether you're in my face or out of my sight.
It hasn't been easy, but I'll never forget it,
because if I didn't live up to your expectations, I would regret it.
There's not a day goes by I don't think of you, or have a memory of you saying the sweet things you used to.
Just know I love and miss you like crazy,
you're forever in my heart and mind Grandma Daisy.

In Loving Memory

Willie Frank Thompson
March 7, 1945 – August 3, 2019

My heart hurts,
I don't even know if my heart really works
I lost someone very close to me,
He is no longer suffering, he's finally free
He was honestly the first man that I ever loved,
I know he's looking down on me, smiling from
heaven above
I miss the laughs and all our long talks,
when I finally say I do, I'll be missing our walk
Life's been pretty lonely without having you here,
It is amazing how much has changed, in just a couple
of years
I shed a few tears daily just thinking about you,
then I smile remembering the fun things we used to
do
I feel like I can face anything now, because nothing
can be harder,
than a daughter who's missing her Father

About The Author

Jacquie C. Hamilton is a native of Greenville, Alabama. She's a mother of three beautiful adult children, a full-time special needs educator and entrepreneur. When Jacquie is not working in the school system, she enjoys volunteering in the community. She is an active member at Indian Hill A.M.E Zion Church, The Order of Eastern Star, and runs her non-profit organization, "Joining Jalen's Fight" in honor of her son who has autism. This organization focuses on sharing stories and providing opportunities to increase understanding and acceptance of people with autism.

Jacquie has learned to thrive by her own motto, "Believe that you deserve it, and the universe will serve it. Get ready for it.

Let's Connect

EMAIL
authorjacquiehamilton@gmail.com

FACEBOOK
@AuthorJacquieHamilton

INSTAGRAM
@jacquie.c.hamilton

www.ingramcontent.com/pod-product-compliance
Lightning Source LLC
Chambersburg PA
CBHW050241010526
44107CB00040B/1478/J